MW00834109

DAG HAMMARSKJÖLD, THE UNITED NATIONS AND THE DECOLONISATION OF AFRICA

HENNING MELBER

Dag Hammarskjöld, the United Nations and the Decolonisation of Africa

OXFORD
UNIVERSITY PRESS

OXFORD

UNIVERSITY PRESS

Oxford University Press is a department of the
University of Oxford. It furthers the University's objective
of excellence in research, scholarship, and education
by publishing worldwide.

Oxford   New York

Auckland   Cape Town   Dar es Salaam   Hong Kong   Karachi
Kuala Lumpur   Madrid   Melbourne   Mexico City   Nairobi
New Delhi   Shanghai   Taipei   Toronto

With offices in

Argentina   Austria   Brazil   Chile   Czech Republic   France   Greece
Guatemala   Hungary   Italy   Japan   Poland   Portugal   Singapore
South Korea   Switzerland   Thailand   Turkey   Ukraine   Vietnam

Oxford is a registered trade mark of Oxford University Press
in the UK and certain other countries.

Published in the United States of America by
Oxford University Press
198 Madison Avenue, New York, NY 10016

Library of Congress Cataloging-in-Publication Data is available
Henning Melber.
Dag Hammarskjöld, the United Nations and the Decolonisation of Africa.
ISBN: 9780190087562

Printed in India on acid-free paper

In memory of
Dag Hammarskjöld (1905–1961)
and
Jean Gazarian (1922–2016)
Knut Hammarskjöld (1922–2012)
Per Lind (1916–2012)
Sture Linnér (1917–2010)
Wilhelm Wachtmeister (1923–2012)
Sverker Åström (1917–2012)

CONTENT

ABOUT THE AUTHOR

HENNING MELBER is Director Emeritus/Senior Advisor of the Dag Hammarskjöld Foundation and former Research Director/Senior Research Associate at the Nordic Africa Institute, both in Uppsala, Sweden. He is Extraordinary Professor in the Department of Political Science of the University of Pretoria and at the Centre for Gender and Africa Studies at the University of the Free State in Bloemfontein; Senior Research Fellow of the Institute of Commonwealth Studies/School of Advanced Study at the University of London; and the President of the European Association of Development Research and Training Institutes (EADI). He has previously published with Hurst, *Understanding Namibia: The Trials of Independence* (2014).

PREFACE

It was at the annual African Studies Conference of the African Studies Association in the UK at Leeds in September 2016. As before on such occasions, I met Michael Dwyer at the Hurst Publishers book display. He asked me about my plans when retiring at the end of October the same year from the Dag Hammarskjöld Foundation. I mentioned that among other things I would like to write an account of Dag Hammarskjöld's role during the initial stages of decolonisation in Africa. Michael nodded and remarked: I will send you a contract. A few days later I realised that he had not been joking ...

Thanks to Michael, I had the opportunity to bring a decade as executive director and senior advisor at the Foundation, which was established 1962 in Hammarskjöld's name, to a kind of scholarly closure. Now I was finally forced to take up a position myself between glorification and castigation of the role the United Nations' second Secretary-General had played while in office between 1953 and 1961. My balancing act is herewith presented to the public for judgement.

Hammarskjöld was not flawless: no human being is. He was aware of his limitations in living up to the values he believed in. But there are few other people whom I admire in a similar way. The only exception perhaps (apart from Sue and Tulinawa, the loves of my life) is Albert Camus, whose photo stands alongside Hammarskjöld's on my desk. For me, both share as their most outstanding feature and conviction the belief that integrity, decency, human dignity, humanism, rights and justice matter. While they lived their short lives in parallel, their paths hardly crossed. They had different visions, but pursued them in similar fashion in an effort to live up to these values in their own lives. For both, a fitting characterisation might be what the poet Carl Sandburg, in a tribute to Abraham Lincoln, called a blend of steel and velvet.

Thank you, Michael, for your trust and confidence, which allowed me to embark on this journey.

Uppsala, Sweden
10 December 2018
(Human Rights Day)

1

INTRODUCTION

HISTORY BETWEEN FACT AND FICTION

The madman shouted in the market place.
No one stopped to answer him.
Thus it was confirmed that his thesis was incontrovertible.[1]

This study seeks to fill a gap in the current literature on the role of the second Secretary-General of the United Nations, who served the institution from 1953 until his death in 1961. Much has already been published on Hammarskjöld. In a pioneering way, Brian Urquhart presented an early insightful account. It is based on his personal interaction with Hammarskjöld and on many documents he had left behind in his office. For a long time, this was the most authoritative study, which focused almost exclusively on the political and diplomatic skills of the Secretary-General.[2] This rather systematic and detailed account was far superior to the many other publications immediately published after Hammarskjöld's death and the years following, which mainly paid him less detailed and more uncritical homage.[3] But Urquhart's comprehensive volume also had its limitations in that it offered the perspectives of someone who was part of the very history he was describing. After all, first-hand accounts of those involved in events are not always the most neutral ones.

The published thesis in German of Manuel Fröhlich, with its much shorter English version, which unfortunately had to sacrifice a lot of the nuanced

1

detail, was able to add important further dimensions.[4] He managed to reconcile the "political" Hammarskjöld with the "spiritual" Hammarskjöld (hardly visible in Urquhart's biography) and included references to Hammarskjöld's "inner world" hitherto largely ignored in the political accounts. These aspects were until recently left all too often to more spiritual—at times esoteric— deliberations not linked to the political role Hammarskjöld had. This literature, while legitimate in its own right, does not play a role in the chapters following. Finally, the biography by Roger Lipsey emphasised in a far more detailed and powerful way than others the synthesis between the socialisation of Hammarskjöld, his career as a Swedish and international civil servant, and his spiritual world, which shaped and guided his ethics and moral values in his diplomacy as well.[5] The complex layers of Hammarskjöld's motives cannot be adequately characterised as "ideology". Rather, they were guiding principles for his convictions and perhaps also served as a moral compass. These interrelated dimensions have largely been deconstructed and dealt with by the three insightful, though not necessarily neutral, analyses of Urquhart, Fröhlich and Lipsey. In their distinct ways they are by far the most intimate engagement with the policies of Hammarskjöld. Their recognition of his role also testifies in very differing ways to their recognition of and admiration for a remarkable person and diplomat.

The variety of aspects that ought to be recognised in a comprehensive assessment of Hammarskjöld's personality and policy, including his often-neglected background as an economist as well as his interest in culture and art, have also been analysed in more detail in many of the contributions to two edited volumes.[6] In addition, the mediation style of Hammarskjöld and his efforts at conflict management are often the subject of peace and security studies. His specific understanding of the role of the Secretary-General as a visionary has also been a subject of comparative studies within the fields of international relations and global governance.[7] Many of the insightful contributions in this area are only mentioned in this book in passing, if at all, since it seeks to fill a gap not covered by them.[8]

In This Book

A lot of (at times rather conflicting) assessments have been presented on Dag Hammarskjöld and the Congo. But beyond this particular case study, Hammarskjöld's more general role in the decolonisation of Africa during the Cold War has been less of a focus.[9] Alanna O'Malley has closed some of the existing gaps, though with a continued emphasis on the Congo.[10] Hammarskjöld and the "Congo Club" also provide a thought-provoking case study within a more principled social analysis of the modus operandi and the underlying social capital of middle-class men in early United Nations peace-building efforts.[11] But there is still a need for an overall contextualisation of Hammarskjöld's role in the decolonisation of Africa within the wider framework of the time and the formative years of the United Nations.

The special attention and prominence given, for understandable reasons, to the Congo (which also plays a prominent role in chapter six of this book) has indirectly contributed to the reduced focus on Hammarskjöld's more general role as regards the entire African continent. As a result, there has not been a wider assessment of his diplomacy and policy as Secretary-General when "the winds of change" (in Harold Macmillan's phrase) were blowing. On a closer look, evidence suggests that Hammarskjöld's support for the independence of African colonies and in particular his role in the Congo were not only increasingly attacked by the Soviet Union. His role was seemingly also less and less appreciated by the dominant Western powers, and he was always despised by the racist minority regimes of southern Africa. His early popularity among the more influential Western governments rapidly declined during his second term in office.

Following these introductory reflections, this study summarises Hammarskjöld's socialisation, background and his understanding of public service as duty as well as his role in the Swedish administration, before facing global policy challenges as the most senior international civil servant (chapter two). Chapter three engages with the United Nations' normative framework as a point of departure for considering Hammarskjöld's terms in office there from 1953 to 1961. Chapter four documents, with reference to many of his speeches, his moral compass in terms of his fundamental conviction about the purpose of the United Nations. How he turned this into a concept of solidarity, an emphasis on the sovereignty of states and the importance of the right to self-determination and development for the decolonisation process emerging on the African continent is the focus of chapter five. The Suez crisis and the intervention in the Congo serve in chapter six as case studies to illustrate Hammarskjöld's efforts to translate values into politics. This is followed by a detailed summary of the investigations following the plane crash near Ndola, where he and fifteen others lost their lives (chapter seven). The concluding chapter eight seeks to give recognition to Hammarskjöld's role in the face of the growing number of more critical assessments of his time in office.

The following pages seek to make the case that his visions were at variance with the interests of the big powers of his time—that he was a kind of "anti-hegemonic" Secretary-General. By doing so, my arguments engage occasionally with some of the more critical assessments that associate him with Western imperialist interests. I offer a more nuanced conclusion: while Hammarskjöld was the product of a Western (Nordic) socialisation, he was at the same time an internationalist whose aspirations were much more far-reaching than promoting a Western agenda in global governance, guided as he was by notions of international solidarity and respect for and recognition of otherness. In doing so, the study assesses Hammarskjöld's space for manoeuvring (or, rather, its limits) and his efforts to recognise what he considered the legitimate interests of the newly independent African states. It shows his strategy to seek close collaboration with the new African as well as other non-aligned states emerging vis-à-vis the power blocs in the East and the West, and also highlights his concept in terms of support for development. This adds further aspects to the ongoing debate, explaining why Hammarskjöld may have been in the way of big power interests and that his untimely death might have been not only a welcome tragedy for many, but the result of active intervention by some.

My aim is at the same time to generate more awareness of the scope as well as the limits of a person's influence and policy in relation to processes within the context of global governance. I focus on the role of the United Nations during this era, its inherent contradictions and challenges, and the limited space for solutions to conflicts, given the essential interests of the big powers during the Cold War. Unfortunately, there remains a lack of African voices and perspectives on record. As a result of such a deficit, the literature tends to document and reflect the mainstream of Western policy of the 1950s vis-à-vis other continents and people. It is not possible in this study to transcend the hegemonic tendency in global governance of the day. Instead, it tries to look in more nuanced detail at how this hegemonic tendency and the space for manoeuvring were dealt with. In this sense it is another "mainstream" contribution. There remains a lot to be done to bring other actors and their voices more adequately into the picture. The decolonisation of Africa, within the limited purpose of this study, remains a predominantly Western affair. But as it tries to show, there were different approaches and options within such Western worldviews and in the thoughts and principles that were translated into policy. By introducing in some detail the inner world and diplomacy of Dag Hammarskjöld (including its limitations when confronted with big power policies) the book seeks to illustrate the kind of choices at hand during these times of the late Western colonial-imperialist world of empire.

Fact or Fiction?

It seems a fair assessment that Dag Hammarskjöld has been "the subject of extensive legend building" in the half a century or so since his death.[12] But legends are not only constructed through a kind of selective heroic narrative by those contemporaries close to him or others in the admiration club.[13] The selective narrative also applies to those with opposite motives, both within the "inner circle" of his time[14] and those since then who describe Hammarskjöld either as a dishonest, opportunistic broker or as the unscrupulous personification of a global governance institution they dismiss as biased and an instrument of imperialism. What has been rightly observed about the "fan club" of Hammarskjöld applies as much to those who launch scathing attacks on his role. Both ignore the complexity of the environment in which he operated, which set limits to individual responsibility: "precious little of this evidence appears to disturb the mostly uncritical and laudatory—sometimes bordering on hagiographical—accounts of Hammarskjöld's ethical approach to diplomacy. In theoretical terms, these oversights prevent a full appreciation of the dilemmas faced by international civil servants in managing the conflicting demands of diverse missions and broad constituencies."[15]

Most of the attempts on both sides—the uncritical "praise songs" as well as the damning "disclosures" debunking the "Hammarskjöld cult"—conveniently ignore the complexity of the man as well as the structures in which he operated. To associate Dag Hammarskjöld with hegemonic policy because the United Nations as an institution of global governance has been constructed in a way that reproduces hegemonic rule is an undue simplification of the dynamics of international organisations. Asymmetrical power relations influencing institutions do not make everyone in such organisations—including the highest international civil servant—by definition an agent of imperialism or of other dominant interests. Someone operating in such environment is still the owner of his or her mind. But at the same time he or she is not protected from being a prisoner of circumstances and at times *Sachzwang* (practical constraint).

I maintain that personal values and integrity do matter, even if they face limitations in the execution of office or other daily practice. It is noteworthy in this regard that few of those who draw conclusions about Hammarskjöld's impact and legacy have bothered to look closely at the numerous statements and speeches of the Secretary-General during his time in office. After all, these fill four edited volumes totalling some 2,000 pages.[16] While there are always discrepancies between what is said and what is done—as so often in politics and diplomacy, and in private life too—these documents offer insights into concepts and convictions and are indicative of Hammarskjöld's values and principles. By repeatedly emphasising them, as he consistently did over eight years in office, they form part of a policy.

As I argue and try to document, Dag Hammarskjöld was indeed a person of integrity, whose moral and political views reflected the humanist spirit of the United Nations Charter which he always considered as the ultimate compass. But given the complexity of matters and the few reliable sources at hand, a final judgement in the absence of verifiable factual evidence risks being speculative. One might, for example, trust or else doubt the degree of "truth" in the following anecdote, shared by one of his assistants at the time:

> In addition to his knowledge, intelligence and efficiency, his most typical characteristic was integrity. He was utterly sensitive to what he saw as any attempt to unduly influence him. A personal experience is the following: During an intermission in a debate in the Security Council, Dag was talking with the British Ambassador Sir Pierson Dixon in the corridor behind the podium. Sir Pierson suggested that the Secretary-General should make a statement in support of the British position. Dag refused. The ambassador insisted that, "After all, there is something called political sense." I stood there together with Dixon's assistant, Douglas Hurd (later to become Mrs. Thatcher's foreign secretary), when Dag, stressing each syllable, declared, "And there is something called integrity," turned around and closed the door behind him.[17]

As this personal memory illustrates, there is all too often a thin line between fact and fiction, which not only this book finds difficult to walk. Is this nice incident recalled by the narrator a true story? Who could verify it, in the absence of any other proof than the witness report? Many of those who have so far engaged with related subjects had either preconceived ideas or a selective approach (and often both, the latter a result of the earlier). Goethe once said that you only know what you see. But the opposite, that you only see what you know, is equally true.

Here are a few more examples, which I came across in the literature, to illustrate the point. When Hammarskjöld is disqualified in a rather dismissive way as being a "Western diplomat", then the only commonsensical response seems to be that of course he was a Western diplomat—what else? And, so what? Used as a kind of predetermination of his values, policy and diplomacy, this is plain nonsense. Western diplomats are not a breed cloned alike and have a variety of options at hand. They should be judged by what they do, not from where they come or what they are supposed and expected to be—after all, they are not doomed by fate or programmed according to a master plan. As for myself, being a white male offers me more often than not undeserved privileges in terms of benefiting without reason or justification from unfair institutionalised discrimination. But this does not imply that by definition I approve of such injustices or that I abuse women or that I am a racist. It does not prevent me from taking sides in social struggles for emancipation with those who are the victims.

Another problem is, as the story about integrity aptly illustrates, the reliability of sources used as evidence to confirm one's assessment. As proof for the conclusion that Hammarskjöld "was in cahoots with the Americans",[18] we are given an internal US intelligence "Synopsis of State and Intelligence Material Reported to the President". It quotes Hammarskjöld as telling the US permanent representative to the UN, Henry Cabot Lodge, that "Lumumba must be 'broken'".[19] However, no matter how often this particular quote is used by critics who see it as ultimate proof of Hammarskjöld's betrayal of declared principles, it is not disclosed who reported this remark, in whose presence it was made, and what purpose it served. It remains a matter of speculation whether this was indeed a reliable verbatim quote, if it was said in a similar way, if it was taken out of context or if it was wishful thinking or a statement made in the belief that President Eisenhower wanted to hear something like this. All we know from eyewitnesses is that Dag Hammarskjöld seemed devastated for days after the news of Lumumba's gruesome torture and murder. We also know from private statements that he considered this an entirely senseless deed.

In a similar vein, the argument has been made (by Nzongola-Ntalaja) that Hammarskjöld shared with other members of his staff "a common Cold War outlook with Western policy makers, and saw their mission in the Congo as that of preserving the then existing balance of forces in the world".[20] To underscore this assessment, Hammarskjöld is quoted as saying that "the Congo should not be permitted to become a Korea, nor should it become a Hungary—or a Munich".[21] One wonders why such a precaution should be used in criticising a policy seeking to keep the Cold War out of the Congo as one of the goals. After all, the scenario would hardly have improved if this had not been achieved, and many of those analysing the Congo crisis of 1960–1, despite differing conclusions and overall judgements, have given Hammarskjöld credit for having managed to secure exactly this. To "reveal Hammarskjöld's pro-West bias", Nzongola-Ntalaja also refers to Rajeshwar Dayal from India, who served as special representative of Hammarskjöld in the Congo, as having reported that the Soviet UN Under-Secretary for Political Affairs, Georgiy Arkadiev, was excluded from all Congo discussions.[22] Commenting on a book under review,[23] Nzongola-Ntalaja then bemoans that its author "is aware of this exclusion and of the American monopoly in the UN Secretary's Congo Club ..., but he does not draw the logical conclusion of UN collusion with U.S. policy".[24] Maybe the author did so because there wasn't sufficient evidence for such collusion, at least when it comes to Dag Hammarskjöld. What Nzongola-Ntalaja does not disclose is Dayal's much more nuanced characterisation of the impasse as a result of personal animosities between Hammarskjöld and Patrice Lumumba, his lack of respect for Arkadiev, and his failure "to develop any understanding with Valerian Zorin" as the Soviet permanent representative, while stressing that this was based on purely individual chemistry and not motivated by fundamental political-ideological differences.[25] After all, as Dayal concludes, "despite occasional failings and misjudgements, history will record the heroic and selfless nature of Hammarskjöld's final service to world peace in the Congo".[26]

As the examples show, misrepresentation to serve a purpose is a temptation we often fail to avoid in our arguments. I am not free from such temptations, while my narrative cannot be described beyond any doubt as fully reliable. One of Hammarskjöld's close Swedish officials on the ground in the Congo recalled in his Dag Hammarskjöld Lecture almost half a century later an exchange with Hammarskjöld over the telephone. The reason was a telegram he had received, threatening "that if Hammarskjöld and his man in the Congo didn't change their pro-Soviet policy, the President [J.F. Kennedy] would see himself obliged to withdraw the US from the UN".[27] Reportedly, when informed, Hammarskjöld retorted over the phone: "I do not intend to give way to any pressure, be it from the East or the West; we shall sink or swim. Continue to follow the line you find to be in accordance with the UN Charter."[28] The story then continues by summarising a meeting with Kennedy in the Oval Room of the White House half a year after Hammarskjöld's death. It claims that the President referred to this incident, explaining the motives for the intervention and that he had since then realised how unjustified it was: "since it was now too late to express his apology to Dag Hammarskjöld, he wanted to do so to me. And the most powerful man in the world added: 'I realise now that in comparison to him, I am a small man. He was the greatest statesman of our century.'"[29]

Here one has to ask to what extent this report is an embellished narrative based on the memory of an old man—a story one wants to tell, to hear and to believe—or a reliable witness statement about something which happened in this or a similar way close enough to reality. What can be verified is the fact that according to the Appointment Book accessible in the Kennedy Library in Boston, Sture Linnér indeed had a meeting on 14 March 1962 at 10.40 a.m. with John F. Kennedy in the presence of Harlan Cleveland, Assistant Secretary of State for International Organizations. But neither the phone call with Hammarskjöld nor the exchange in the Oval Office was reliably recorded.

In contrast, there is a major source that can provide a fair assessment of Hammarskjöld's approach. The collected four volumes of the statements and speeches of Hammarskjöld during his eight years in office remain a reliable body of evidence of his analyses and arguments, at the same time indicating his convictions—unless one is convinced that this is the testimony of a notorious liar, who managed to mislead the world. This book therefore uses often this source to convey Hammarskjöld's approach in his own words, even at the risk of quoting lengthy passages from the original.

Readers are invited to judge their own feelings and conclusions at the end of the book, to which version of Hammarskjöld's role as Secretary-General of the United Nations they tend. I confess upfront that while I do not consider the main actor in the following chapters as flawless, I continue to admire his values, principles and integrity, despite the situations in which he seemingly failed. Nobody is perfect: why should Hammarskjöld have been so?

Finally, there are other questions which readers should keep in mind when engaging with the arguments of this book. What might have happened if Hammarskjöld and the United Nations had not intervened in the Suez crisis? Would the people of the Congo have been better off without the United Nations peacekeeping force and Hammarskjöld? Would it have been better not to "leave it to Dag"? I hope that the pages that follow will make it easier to find answers to questions like these.

2

SERVICE AS DUTY

DAG HAMMARSKJÖLD'S UPBRINGING, ETHICS, AND EARLY CAREER

Never look down to test the ground before taking your next step: only he who keeps his eye fixed on the far horizon will find his right road.[1]

Life only demands from you the strength you possess. Only one feat is possible—not to have run away.[2]

Dag Hjalmar Agne Carl Hammarskjöld was born on 29 July 1905 in the Swedish town of Jönköping, the youngest of four sons of Agnes (1867–1940) and Hjalmar (1862–1953). At the time of his birth, his father—previously law professor at Uppsala University, Minister of Justice (1901–2) and Minister of Ecclesiastical Affairs (1904–5)—was away, heading the delegation negotiating Norwegian independence. Appointed governor of the Uppland region in 1907, he moved with his family to Uppsala. While carrying out this office until 1930, he was also appointed as Prime Minister by the Swedish King in 1914 for an interim period. His World War I policy of strict neutrality caused food shortages and massive protest among the population, earning him the name "Hungerskjöld". Under pressure and politically isolated, he resigned in 1917. He was elected to the Swedish Academy in 1918 and chaired the Nobel Foundation from 1929 to 1947. Among other assignments and prestigious offices, he was president of the Academy of International Law at The Hague (1924–38). Hjalmar Hammarskjöld died half a year after his son was appointed as second Secretary-General of the United Nations. Dag succeeded his father in 1954, when he was elected to his vacant chair at the Swedish Academy, which awards the annual Nobel Prize for Literature.[3]

Raised in the awakening ecumenical spirit of Uppsala, the seat of the Church of Sweden, and strongly influenced by personal encounters with Bishop Nathan Söderblom[4] and Albert Schweitzer, Dag was familiar with a wider world of faith, embracing tolerance and respect for others. His affinity with the world of both religion and the muses may have been more the result of his mother's influence. She came from the Almquist family with its literary tradition and had a close bond with Dag, her youngest son.[5]

Although father and son (unlike mother and son) had a rather distant relationship,

> Hjalmar Hammarskjöld had a profound influence on how his son understood his duties as a civil servant. Dag, like his father, would constantly struggle to conform to the ideal of the unbiased official ... He always strove to find a position, based on legal principles and not on *Realpolitik*, which would allow decisions to be made regardless of political or national pressures. At the age of 25, Dag wrote prophetically to an old friend: "[My father] and I think differently about most things and yet, my standpoints—in the most serious meaning of the word—build upon his, in every way."[6]

Known as a man of firm principles, Hjalmar Hammarskjöld had put these principles above any opportunistic behaviour that sought popularity. He likewise expected from his sons the highest service to the country, understood as serving the best interests of the people, the Swedish *folket*. Civil service in Sweden had a long tradition of selfless duty dedicated to the public benefit of ordinary citizens.

For his son Dag, who was also measured against the career of two of his older brothers,[7] the uncompromising ethics of life as a duty to serve in the best interests of the people and thereby humanity, bordered at times on a painful soul-searching journey into the unknown within him. As we know from his entries in his private notebook which he started to write in 1925, he was a deeply spiritual individual inspired by the mystics, while at the same time influenced by the Protestant ethic of service to humanity.[8] Among his earliest entries—made between 1925 and 1930—were the two introductory quotes to this chapter. The strong belief in determination and perseverance expressed there was programmatic for all his life.

At Uppsala University, the multilingual Dag Hammarskjöld (he soon became fluent in English, French and German and cultivated a remarkably poetic

Swedish) obtained a Bachelor of Arts degree in 1925 and majored in Economics in 1928. He completed a Bachelor of Law degree in 1930.[9] He then relocated with his parents to Stockholm, entered a career in the civil service and finally obtained a doctoral degree in Economics at Stockholm University in 1933, with Gunnar Myrdal as his opponent at his public examination. Despite many differences in their approaches (Hammarskjöld was mainly a follower of Keynesian economic policy), both subsequently collaborated for decades in the Swedish government and later in the United Nations.[10]

Although he was never a member of any political party, Hammarskjöld built a comet-like career in government. As a high-ranking civil servant, he was highly influential in economic and fiscal policy matters in the Swedish social democratic governments.[11] From 1936 to 1945 he was undersecretary in the Finance Ministry and from 1941 to 1948 chairperson of the Swedish central bank's board of governors. Having the confidence and trust of Ernst Wigforss,[12] he was one of the architects of the welfare state and drafted the bill for long-term fiscal policy in 1946. "In his memoirs, Wigforss testifies to his close relationship with Hammarskjöld: 'Agreement between us was far more conspicuous than our differences. Had it not been so our collaboration would scarcely have endured for ten years,' he writes, and adds: 'The truth is the finance policy we pursued was as much his as mine.'"[13]

In 1946, the position of senior economic advisor was specially created for him when joining the Ministry for Foreign Affairs under Östen Undén,[14] where he dealt internationally with the economic problems Sweden was facing at the time. From 1947 he was the main negotiator in international economic affairs, being involved in the administration of the Marshall Plan and in setting up the Committee of European Economic Co-operation (CEEC), later the OECD. He became a cabinet minister without portfolio in 1951, remained a delegate to the CEEC, and headed the Swedish Mission at the United Nations in 1952–1953. As a cabinet minister without party membership, Hammarskjöld felt accountable to a wider public in respect of his views on current matters. He made these views known by means of three articles published in 1951–1952: two in a social democratic and one in a conservative journal.

In the first article, published in the periodical *Tiden* (*Time*), he discussed his role as a government official and gave a candid account of his general political philosophy.

> Referring to Albert Schweitzer's ethical precept, "reverence for life", he distinguished three aspects, or traits, in his political make-up: a "conservative" side, born of respect for our historical heritage; a "liberal, social radical side", reflect-

ing his belief not only in the right of the individual to live his or her life according to his or her conscience, but also in social justice, that is equal rights and opportunities for all; and, finally, the "self-evident subordination of one's own interest to the whole". The last trait, he explained, involved a moral duty—loyalty to one's country. But Hammarskjöld also meant it to be understood as loyalty to "the wider view of society embodied in internationalism".[15]

Hammarskjöld's faith had many sources of inspiration, including rather worldly ones. He was deeply imbued with the values of Swedish society of the 1930s and 1940s. In the tradition of the Swedish civil service, holding office was not supposed to mean serving the state as detached from the people, but rather serving the community of citizens. This implied an ethos of inner autonomy and independence guided by integrity. Based on fundamental Christian principles, loyalty to the law was understood as faithful service, with conscience as a moral compass, aimed at the general welfare and public benefit. In an ideal sense, this required him to represent not public power but public virtue, and to observe a pragmatism based on firm principles.

Swedish policy of the 1930s was guided by the desire to establish a social contract between capital and labour, mediated by the state, to promote a social welfare economy. Political scientists have called this consociational democracy. It is a consensus-seeking approach seeking to find shared interests among potentially antagonistic social forces with the aim of achieving a sustainable basis for policy implementation serving the interests of all. In the Swedish case, this meant the promotion of social welfare as an investment in political stability. Such an approach required particular mediation techniques and skills, involving the widest possible consultation to bring all parties on board. This consensus-seeking policy excluded blind obedience towards the authority of the state, and sought agreement between parties rather than imposing policy. It required what Hammarskjöld called a "maturity of mind".[16]

But such maturity had its limitations, especially when Hammarskjöld was of the conviction that what he believed in was right and that he knew what was wrong. This could have been understood as self-righteousness, stubbornness or aloofness during negotiations in stressful situations. At the same time, this strong sense of belonging allowed him to enter new territory with an open mind and curiosity. After all, the better one is anchored in one's own identity, the more one can afford to engage with real or perceived "otherness". When departing from Stockholm for New York, a journalist enquired if he would continue as Secretary-General to speak as a Swede or only as an international citizen of the world. He responded that he would of course speak as a Swede in the sense that one is not uprooted from one's home ground when entering an international office.[17]

The obligation to serve the greater public good during one's professional life was a guiding principle in the ranks of the higher public servants of his time, which Hammarskjöld had internalised. One of the core values of Swedish society of this time was represented by the term *anständighet*, which is only partly captured in the word "decency" in combination with "prowess". When he was one of the highest-ranking members in the Swedish state administration, he made an entry in 1950 in his notebook: "A modest wish: that our doings and dealings may be of a little more significance to life than a man's dinner jacket to his digestion. Yet not a little of what we describe as our achievement is, in fact, no more than a garment in which, on festive occasions, we seek to hide our nakedness."[18]

His personal reflections were only discovered after his death. He left the notes behind together with a letter in which he described them as "a sort of *white book* concerning my negotiations with myself—and with God".[19] The entries reveal his radical self-criticism and constant interrogation as regards the temptations in life: "On his search for universalization, Hammarskjöld drew from his personal mystic, with its basic concepts of love, patience, justice and prudence, to concrete political activity."[20] The publication of his reflections provoked confusion, irritation, at times shock and dismay, if not scorn, within Swedish society, which had become strongly secular and in part deeply suspicious of any metaphysical sphere or spirituality.[21]

While many have dismissed his inner conversations as escapism, others consider them as useful insights that explain some of his values and principles in more depth. Some of the entries have been interpreted as reflections or even mirror images of the secular challenges he was facing.[22] Another important dimension of Hammarskjöld's value system, which can be fully understood only through his negotiations with himself and with God, has been highlighted in a social analysis of the pioneers of United Nations peacebuilding initiatives. It refers to Hammarskjöld as a prime example of nineteenth-century European *Bürgerlichkeit*, recalling Max Weber's analysis of the Protestant ethic:

> According to Weber, Protestants and capitalists alike profoundly believe that true human fulfilment has to be realized through unquestioning efficiency, no matter the professional activity or the challenges imposed. Weber's German term is *Tüchtigkeit*, the meaning of which actually goes beyond efficiency. *Tüchtigkeit* not only designates the thoroughness and reliability with which a

certain task is completed, but also the relentless willingness to take up any challenge, no matter how onerous, time-consuming, or difficult its achievement will be. Work becomes a calling, an ethical duty, and not merely a means to gain one's own daily bread; ... professional efficiency is an end in itself for liberals and Protestants; it has its own beauty and worth. Hammarskjöld's life was fundamentally dominated by this core idea of duty-fulfillment.[23]

This seems a valid observation. But one should avoid end up with the simplifying equation that reduces the Protestant ethic to a set of norms and orientations applicable only to capitalism or capitalist systems. Ethics of such calibre (like most ethics shaped by religion, culture and modes of production) may be the result of certain socio-economic processes and the impact of their reproduction on mentalities and mindsets. Lutheran and Calvinist theologies illustrate very well some shifts that took place in early capitalist societies.[24] But a worldview like the Protestant ethic should not be considered as serving only an instrumentalist function. Those who have internalised and live such ethics do have choices about whom to serve and how. This is apparent in the era of Enlightenment, which produced a justifying legitimacy for the expansion of "Western civilisation" and at the same time it produced thinkers who were fundamentally opposed to such hegemonic ideas and challenged some of the dominant ideological justifications for inequality and injustice.[25]

Although one's convictions may have been moulded in a certain social context, this does not eliminate the possibility of individual choices. No value system can turn individuals into brainless robots without empathy and moral as well as political choices. Humans may be shaped by their socialisation, but are not predetermined in an absolute way, if "conscience", "decency" and "integrity" have any real meaning. People can choose alternatives or make independent decisions, albeit limited by the circumstances in which they find themselves. This also applies to the ways the Protestant ethic is translated into policy and practice. Applying it so as to contribute towards building a welfare state, as Hammarskjöld did during his early career as a Swedish civil servant, was not a bad choice to begin with.

3

THE UNITED NATIONS BETWEEN EMPIRE
AND EMANCIPATION

The purposes of the United Nations are:

2. To develop friendly relations among nations based on respect for the principle of equal rights and self-determination of peoples, and to take other appropriate measures to strengthen universal peace ...[1]

Some 51 representatives of states signed the Charter of the United Nations on 26 June 1945 in San Francisco at the conclusion of the United Nations Conference on International Organization. It came into force on 24 October the same year. The composition of those establishing the successor body to the League of Nations illustrated the political situation at the end of World War II. "We the Peoples of the United Nations", as the Preamble starts, declared their intention "to employ international machinery for the promotion of the economic and social advancement of all peoples". Their respective governments were authorised to sign the following 19 chapters with a total of 107 articles to "hereby establish an international organization to be known as the United Nations". The peoples represented then (or at least parts of them) through the governments in attendance included Egypt, Ethiopia, Liberia and South Africa as the only four sovereign African states. That governments did not necessarily represent the majority of the people in their countries could not be better illustrated than the case of the South African white minority regime practising apartheid at home.

Self-Determination, Human Rights and Decolonisation

It is noteworthy that the preceding Atlantic Charter, signed on 14 August 1941 between President F.D. Roosevelt and Prime Minister Winston Churchill, included, in the sixth of the eight guiding principles for a post-war global order, the "hope to see established a peace which will afford to all nations the means of dwelling in safety within their own boundaries, and which will afford assurance that all the men in all the lands may live out their lives in freedom from fear and want".[2] Not only were women subsumed under men—a sign of the times—the all-embracing language lasting throughout the 1950s and beyond.[3] The statement also implicitly equated nations and their boundaries with the states in existence. Subjects in the colonial territories were not seen as qualifying—though subsequently a debate over the meaning and scope of self-determination did discuss the extent to which the Atlantic Charter actually—if only unintentionally—paved the way into such uncharted territory.[4] After all, Churchill was on record as saying that he "did not become the Prime Minister of Her Majesty's Government in order to preside over the liquidation of the British Empire".[5] Not surprisingly, therefore, the representatives of the colonial states at San Francisco were anxious to keep control over a world of empires, albeit with an uneasy feeling of reassurance: "Even if the idea of an all-encompassing system of trusteeship failed to take hold at San Francisco, the notion that the UN could still play an important role ... would have important ramifications for the evolution—and ultimate demise—of colonial empires in the late 1940s and 1950s."[6]

The UN Charter was to a certain extent ambiguous and reflected a two-pronged approach to colonialism. Article 1 in Chapter 1 ("Purposes and Principles") left a wide space open for interpretation as regards territories under foreign rule by declaring:

2. To develop friendly relations among nations based on respect for the principle of equal rights and self-determination of peoples, and to take other appropriate measures to strengthen universal peace;

3. To achieve international co-operation in solving international problems of an economic, social, cultural, or humanitarian character, and in promoting and encouraging respect for human rights and for fundamental freedoms for all without distinction as to race, sex, language, or religion; and

4. To be a centre for harmonizing the actions of nations in the attainment of these common ends.

In contrast to the wide definition of "self-determination of peoples" and "fundamental freedoms for all", Chapters XII (International Trusteeship

System, Articles 75 to 85) and XIII (The Trusteeship Council, Articles 86 to 91) strictly speaking provided the UN with no authority to interfere with existing colonies. The Trusteeship Council only had formal responsibility for those territories with mandates established under the League of Nations, those detached from Germany and Japan after World War II, and those placed under the system voluntarily by states that held administrative responsibility for them (Article 77).[7] However, the preceding Chapter XI (Declaration Regarding Non-Self-Governing Territories) offered a loophole for those advocating and articulating the demand for independence of the colonies. As Article 73 stated:

> Members of the United Nations which have or assume responsibilities for the administration of territories whose people have not yet attained a full measure of self-government recognize the principle that the interests of the inhabitants of these territories are paramount, and accept as a sacred trust the obligation to promote to the utmost ... the well-being of the inhabitants of these territories, and to this end:
>
> a. to ensure, with due respect for the culture of the peoples concerned, their political, economic, social, and educational advancement, their just treatment, and their protection against abuses;
> b. to develop self-government, to take due account of the political aspirations of the people, and to assist them in the progressive development of their free political institutions, according to the particular circumstances of each territory and its peoples and their varying stages of advancement;
> c. to further international peace and security;
> d. to promote constructive measures of development, to encourage research, and to co-operate with one another and, when and where appropriate, with specialized international bodies with a view to the practical achievement of the social, economic and scientific purposes set forth in this Article; and
> e. to transmit regularly to the Secretary-General for information purposes, subject to such limitations as security and constitutional considerations may require, statistical and other information of a technical nature relating to economic, social, and educational conditions in the territories for which they are respectively responsible other than those territories to which Chapters XII and XIII apply.

This offered "a significant opening that allowed people across the world to see into the inner lives of those empires".[8] The reluctance of the colonial powers to comply with the defined obligations, and their failure to present data which could satisfy the specified goals, provided opportunities to advance the case against colonialism. European empires were increasingly taken to task by those member states who were willing to place the matter on the agenda—and their number increased with every former colony that joined the organisation. The growth of anticolonial forces marked

> a steady shift of active concern with colonial problems from the Trusteeship Council to the General Assembly. The Assembly during this period [1946 to 1960] took the Trusteeship Council to task for its timidity in dealing with the colonial powers. The Assembly also did not hesitate to consider colonial disputes which the Security Council dodged. Thus, by the start of 1960 the Assembly through a decade and a half of active, probing concern with colonial problems had established for itself a dominant position in the Organization with respect to these problems.[9]

At the same time, the Trusteeship Council's originally limited authority was considerably expanded: "the significant number of petitions and the obligation by the Council to examine them in consultation with the administering member state would, to a large extent, promote the cause of decolonisation".[10] The Charter of the United Nations in actual effect paved the way towards decolonisation. In addition, the Universal Declaration of Human Rights, adopted by the United Nations General Assembly in Paris on 10 December 1948, offered another reference point.[11] The Preamble declared a number of principles "as a common standard of achievement for all peoples and all nations ... to secure their universal and effective recognition and observance, both among the peoples of Member States themselves and among the peoples of territories under their jurisdiction". According to Article 2:

> Everyone is entitled to all the rights and freedoms set forth in the Declaration, without distinction of any kind, such as race, colour, sex, language, religion, political or other opinion, national or social origin, property, birth or other status. Furthermore, no distinction shall be made on the basis of the political, jurisdictional or international status of the country or territory to which a person belongs, whether it be independent, trust, non-self-governing or under any other limitation of sovereignty.

This strengthened efforts to name and shame the violation of fundamental rights under colonial rule. "To the extent that the European powers were committed to it, it was important for the colonized to infuse the *Declaration* with ideas that would make it appear incompatible with segregation and colonialism."[12] Human rights abuses served as an important marker for increasing pressure on the mandatory powers to challenge their trusteeship and, by implication, the justification of foreign colonial rule more generally. As a result, "The object of human rights eventually became synonymous with the emerging Third World's concerns over ending colonialism and colonialist practices."[13] Soon member states used the General Assembly, dubbed "the closest thing we have to a 'global conscience'",[14] to influence the norm-setting agenda and its interpretation. Resolution 637(VII), adopted on 16 December 1952, sought to "recognize and promote the realization of the right of self-determination of the peoples of Non-Self-Governing and Trust Territories".[15] In this way it went a step further than the Charter, by linking self-determination of peoples to the Charter's chapters on trusteeship: "With a single resolution, the Assembly changed the objective of 'advancement' into that of 'self-determination', overruling the tortuous compromise reached after the difficult discussions in San Francisco."[16]

Despite such entry points created through the normative frameworks established, it required the continued advocacy of the African, Arab and Asian countries throughout the 1950s to advance their views within the global organisation. A turning point for the United Nations as a collective voice was the Asian-African Conference in the Indonesian city of Bandung (since then dubbed the Bandung Conference) from 18 to 24 April 1955.[17] Among the thirty countries participating were Egypt, Ethiopia, Liberia and Sudan as well as a delegation from the Gold Coast (later Ghana).[18] The conference was "fired with anti-colonial zeal ... to challenge a global order still infused with racist hierarchy and imperialism"[19] and it became the pioneering forerunner of the Non-Aligned Movement. Revealingly, the very first item on the agenda of the Political Committee was "human rights and self-determination". The intense discussions revealed differences in the endorsement of the United Nations Charter as well as the Human Rights Declaration.[20] The compromise was to mention both, but only with the declared "full support" of the Charter.[21] The clause in the final communiqué stressed the linkage between self-determination and sovereignty—understood as decolonisation—on the one hand and the notion of human rights on the other:

C. Human rights and self-determination.

1. The Asian-African Conference declared its full support of the fundamental principles of Human Rights as set forth in the Charter of the United Nations and took note of the Universal Declaration of Human Rights as a common standard of achievement for all peoples and all nations.

The Conference declared its full support of the principle of self-determination of peoples and nations as set forth in the Charter of the United Nations and took note of the United Nations resolutions on the rights of peoples and nations to self-determination, which is a pre-requisite of the full enjoyment of all fundamental Human Rights.[22]

The declaration testified to a new role for non-Western countries: "While norms related to anticolonialism, nonintervention, universal collective security, and human rights predated it, the Bandung Conference sought to enhance their legitimacy."[23] By doing so, its signatories collectively displayed "a normative agency—for example an ability to interpret, localise, formulate and strengthen the rules of international order to advance freedom, peace and order".[24]

After Bandung, the number of newly independent states increased rapidly. By 1961, member states of the United Nations had more than doubled from 51 to 104. In total, 25 independent African countries joined during the period when Dag Hammarskjöld was in office as Secretary-General (1953–1961), with six during the 1950s in the following order: Libya (1955), Morocco, Sudan and Tunisia (1956), Ghana (1957) and Guinea (1958). Finally, 1960 was the year when British Prime Minister Harold Macmillan observed in a speech in the South African parliament on 3 February: "The wind of change is blowing through this continent, and whether we like it or not, this growth of national consciousness is a political fact. We must all accept it as a fact, and our national policies must take account of it."[25] In that year Dahomey (now Benin), Upper Volta (now Burkina Faso), Cameroon, the Central African Republic, Chad, Congo (Brazzaville), Coté d'Ivoire, Congo (Kinshasa), Gabon, Madagascar, Mali, Niger, Nigeria, Senegal, Somalia and Togo—in total, 16 states—declared their independence, followed in 1961 by Mauritania, Sierra Leone and today's Tanzania. This shifted the balance in the General Assembly, as new members were able to create and occupy new space. As a result, the Declaration on the Granting of Independence to Colonial Countries and People was adopted as General Assembly Resolution 1514(XV) on 14 December 1960, stating:

1. The subjection of peoples to alien subjugation, domination and exploitation constitutes a denial of fundamental human rights, is contrary to the Charter of the United Nations and is an impediment to the provision of world peace and cooperation.
2. All peoples have the right to self-determination; by virtue of that right they freely determine their political status and freely pursue their economic, social and cultural development.[26]

Adopted by 89 member states with no vote against and nine abstentions (by Australia, Belgium, the Dominican Republic, Great Britain, France, Portugal, South Africa, Spain and the United States), this "proved to be an epochal document that heralded the end of colonialism ... endowed with a high moral authority".[27] While it took at least another three decades until colonialism indeed became history, Resolution 1514 marked a turning point and a victory for those who during the 1950s mobilised for the right to self-determination.

It has been said that "Where the world body's role as a collective imperialist ended and its role as an ally of liberation began was not always easy to ascertain."[28] More certain is that the time span of 15 years had created a modified landscape in international relations, which—at least nominally and within the limited manoeuvring space of the General Assembly—provided the new states with a forum to promote their perspectives vis-à-vis those holding the ultimate power of definition as permanent members of the Security Council.

The Normative and Political Power of Rights Discourses

As I have suggested, the Charter and subsequent resolutions and declarations helped promote the struggle for self-determination, anti-colonialism and human rights in the sense that these linkages "demonstrate the mutual impact of the histories of international human rights and decolonization". Their connectivity contributed to "the making of a human rights regime".[29] Of late, there has been criticism of those who maintain such an evolutionary perspective. While it is conceded "that postcolonial actors decisively shaped UN human rights work", it is argued that "in the process leading to the end of colonialism, human rights were neither highly significant nor completely absent".[30] Rather, human rights claims served an instrumental purpose, "and those activists making use of them engaged in a distinct appropriation of the idea for highly politicized ends".[31] It would be more surprising if a human rights discourse had not become highly politicised. After all, normative frameworks, and in particular the notion of human rights and related discourses, tend to be political by nature, once they become a matter of contestation. It therefore seems rather provocative to suggest that "anticolonialism wasn't a human rights movement".[32] One critic, Samuel Moyn, even goes a step further by suggesting that the United Nations during the 1950s and 1960s was "responsible for the irrelevance of human rights".[33] For him, human rights only entered the global setting in a meaningful way from the 1970s, not least through the role played by US President Jimmy Carter. Moyn insists that the Universal Declaration of Human Rights was not as important a marker as some believe, and that "human rights in their specific contemporary connotations are an invention of recent date".[34] But the argument at the same time partly confirms the commonly held idea that the human rights debate acquires specific connotations according to when, where and over which issues it takes place. So it does not convincingly discredit the view that human rights mattered in the specific context of the 1950s when discussing colonialism and self-determination. The dismissive undertone downplays the relevance that normative frameworks had had, since the adoption of the United Nations Charter and the Universal Declaration of Human Rights for the anti-colonial movements and their supporters, as a "source of embarrassment" which could be used against the colonial powers.[35]

In a similar vein, Mark Mazower tends to downplay the impact that the early normative frameworks of the United Nations had for the anti-colonial movements. For him, their continuing global dominance enabled the Western powers to reinvent the League of Nations after World War II to anchor and reproduce their control over international affairs.[36] The norms created reflected existing power relations and, by implication, the authority to decide when, where and how they were applied. Global governance as institutionalised by the United Nations "involves the establishment of a 'civilising' standard demarcating the west, which imposes, from the rest, which is imposed upon".[37] In such a perspective, the dynamics we have documented are neglected if not ignored. Not by accident, perhaps, the codification of international human rights law and the related principles of self-determination hardly feature at all in Mazower's study. But while they were designed in a purely Western perspective of Empire, they could subsequently be turned against those creating them. Mazower's argument, that "although the UN could shine a bright light of publicity on colonial rule, it lacked the military force necessary to enforce its own policies",[38] does not question that the discussion initiated in the United Nations brought the issue into prominence and thereby ultimately contributed to changing the situation.

Interestingly, an earlier study of Mazower illustrated the point, albeit unintentionally, that normative markers originally conceived according to one perspective could be turned in favour of those advocating a different meaning. Offering "a series of probes into the ideological prehistory of the United Nations and the postwar world order",[39] he presented the organisation "as essentially a further chapter in the history of world organisation inaugurated by the League and linked through that to the question of empire and the visions of global order that emerged out of the British empire in particular in its final decades".[40] But, as he also admits, while "there is much plausibility in the idea that the UN was designed by, and largely operated as an instrument of, great power politics ... this is not the whole story by any means".[41]

Mazower uses four chapters to introduce individual protagonists of specific issues. By contrasting the South African Jan Smuts as a co-founder of both the League and the United Nations (chapter 1) with Jawaharlal Nehru from India (chapter 4), he puts into question his own main hypothesis of continuing Western normative power. Suggesting "that the United Nations started out life not as the instrument to end colonialism, but rather ... as the means to preserve it", he says that the defeat which Smuts suffered at the hands of India at the United Nations illustrates "the rise and fall of the idea of an imperial internationalism".[42] Already during the first decade of the world body's existence "the principle of national self-determination was globalized in a startlingly rapid fashion, and the UN turned from being an instrument of empire into an anti-colonial forum".[43]

Ironically, Smuts played a decisive role in introducing "human rights" as a category into the language—and subsequent politics—of the United Nations, which the Charter turned into binding law and legal obligation for the member states. Attending the first meeting of the General Assembly in October 1946 in New York, the Indian delegation (not yet representing a sovereign state) reminded Smuts of his own credo—only to condemn South Africa's racial policy against the country's Indian minority (not the black majority) as a human rights violation. Smuts's argument, that this was a purely domestic affair in which other states had no right to interfere, did not prevent his humiliating defeat. The General Assembly not only condemned South Africa for its treatment of Indians but also rejected the South African request for the incorporation of neighbouring South West Africa, a former German colony administered by South Africa as a C Mandate since the end of World War I, by 37 votes to 9.[44]

Mazower does recognise this success in turning the key notion of human rights, introduced by Smuts, against his own country's policy as "the first act of assertion by the colonial world against the principles of racial hierarchy and European rule"[45]—at a time when the colonial world still had hardly any agency or voice at the General Assembly. Thereby, "Smuts was the first casualty of the new system that he had helped to create, and he admitted sardonically that he was exposed as a 'hypocrite'".[46] His "conception of 'freedom' was not synonymous with political equality", and he had not anticipated "how rapidly and extensively, and, in many ways, how differently from his vision, human rights would evolve to attempt to address the needs of an era to which he did not belong".[47] Using this case as an ample illustration, Heyns and Gravett suggest:

> States did not sign a blank cheque in San Francisco by adopting the Charter as far as the meaning and content of human rights were concerned. In many respects it was left open for later determination, also by those states who were

not major powers at the time, including those which were in the process of decolonization. These unintended consequences of the process that he initiated Smuts would soon enough see in action for himself.

...

It was clear that the new world organization would not confine itself to the restricted vision of its founders. The human rights provisions of the Charter would acquire a life of their own.[48]

As a more general conclusion, Heyns and Gravett consider this as an early example of "a deep duality in the international order", characteristic of the dualistic nature of the human rights project, which "does not represent an objective order and is not neutral; like law in general, international law represents a nexus of power relations and value judgments. At best, it is a fusion of the self-interest of its creators and a measure of idealism ... Smuts' duality is a particularly visible manifestation."[49] Such dualism signifies "the fault line that runs through international law and relations, and indeed probably the human personality".[50] The stages and forms of contestation over the content, phrasing, definition and applicability of the Charter, the Universal Declaration of Human Rights and subsequent normative frameworks are fascinating as examples. They show that even from the margins the "South" was very soon able to enter the battles over ownership and make use of the new forums and platforms to articulate and promote their desires and demands—if only also to forget about the values and principles used as handy arguments for the legitimacy of the struggle for emancipation, once independence had been achieved back home. Opportunism and selectivity are among the most universal traits of rulers, as diverse as these might be. But that is another story for another book. For the purpose of this one, the reflections of a former permanent representative of South Africa to the United Nations capture the Southern perspectives very well as regards the role of the global body, based on its track record since the 1950s: "It serves as a beacon of hope and inspiration for the poor, disadvantaged, and marginalised peoples of the world. It is also a centre for the political co-ordination of liberation efforts, and the font of many of the international laws and norms on which those who are involved in struggles for liberation and independence can draw their strength and legitimacy."[51]

In contrast to this view, it has become *en vogue* to present a sceptical if not outright negative conclusion about the relevance of the United Nations and its potential for contributing to reform and change, based on human rights, in the societies of our world. But as this chapter suggests, the United Nations, as "the endgame of empire",[52] created the space for counter-narratives and empowered, at least on certain occasions and in specific constellations, those who were supposed to remain on the receiving end. As Mazower also illustrated through his focus on the role of individuals in setting norms and their interpretations, the personal is political—and it matters even on the level of global governance. Enter Dag Hammarskjöld.

4

DAG HAMMARSKJÖLD'S CREDO
AND THE UNITED NATIONS

*It has been said that the United Nations was not created in order to bring us to
heaven, but in order to save us from hell. I think that sums up as well as anything I
have heard both the essential role of the United Nations and the attitude of mind
that we should bring to its support.*[1]

It would be wrong to assume that Dag Hammarskjöld entered terra incognita
when assuming office as Secretary-General. As the debates on the meaning of
the Charter show, there had already been conflict about the interpretation of
norms as well as the institutional structures and roles of the global governance
body. His predecessor, the Norwegian Trygve Lie, had for seven years been
engaged in—and mainly lost—battles over the meaning and influence of the
position of Secretary-General of which he was the first incumbent.[2] His performance has not been rated very favourably. But, as suggested, he actually
paved the way for his successor's fights for a proactive office:

> Despite the failure of Lie's specific initiatives, his activities created precedents
> for the SG's role that amounted to an expansion in a political direction. Even
> failed initiatives may lead to institutional change ... Lie explored the role of the
> SG as an advocate for global issues, or as he called it a "spokesman for the world
> interest". He strengthened the position of the SG as representing the UN and
> being a guardian of the UN Charter.[3]

Already in December 1945 the report of the United Nations Preparatory
Commission "noted the SG's symbolic role as it talked about his 'moral

authority' and stated that 'the Secretary-General, more than anyone else, will stand for the United Nations as a whole'".[4] The report granted—maybe much more than the big powers were actually willing to concede—influence and leverage to the highest international civil servant. As one of the assessments of the role of the Secretary-General sensibly observed: "Good faith, honesty, truth telling—all the old-fashioned virtues—can become tools of peacemaking in the hands of the secretaries-general, especially if they are perceived as using those qualities in the service of some greater good."[5] At the same time, assuming such authority and trying to execute it meant having to manoeuvre between Scylla and Charybdis in view of the rift that had emerged between the big powers with the dawn of the Cold War. Trygve Lie was the first victim of such a polarised divide in world politics. While he was re-elected for a second term in November 1950, he subsequently lost the support of the Soviet Union over the Korea War. The boycott of his office forced him ultimately to resign on 10 November 1952.[6] Based on his experiences, he remarked in his memoirs: "When he agrees with us, governments tend to feel, the Secretary-General is within his rights, and is a good fellow besides; when his views differ from ours he clearly is exceeding his authority, his reasoning is bad, and even his motives may be suspect."[7] A recent reappraisal of his role has pointed out that, despite being largely forgotten or ignored, "Lie was instrumental in expanding the role of the SG in a political direction".[8]

The Unknown Swede

Since experience of a Secretary-General assuming political responsibilities in his office had created concerns, it took the permanent members of the Security Council several months before they could agree on a successor. Finally, after failing in a first round to secure acceptance of one of three candidates put to the vote in the Security Council in March 1953, a shortlist of four names was circulated. It included the largely unknown Dag Hammarskjöld, minister in the Swedish Foreign Office, who was the head of his country's delegation at the General Assembly in 1952. Ironically, Hammarskjöld became the candidate of choice because he was widely considered to be an apolitical bureaucrat. According to Brian Urquhart, one of the first international civil servants in the Secretary-General's office, Trygve Lie strongly opposed Hammarskjöld's appointment because "he would be no more than a clerk".[9] Carl Schürmann, the long-serving representative of the Netherlands, recalled:

> In spite of the reputation of ability and integrity which he had acquired among those who had met him in negotiations or at conferences, it cannot be said that

he was, at that moment, the obvious candidate for this high international function. His election was much more due to the wish of the Big Powers to see— after Trygve Lie who had taken a strong position in several questions—at the head of the Secretariat someone who would concentrate mainly on the administrative problems and who would abstain from public statements on the political conduct of the Organization. Such a careful and colourless official they thought to have found in Dag Hammarskjöld.[10]

When confronted with the completely unexpected news of his selection, Hammarskjöld was initially reluctant. After consultations with the Swedish Prime Minister and the Foreign Minister and his release from Cabinet, he visited his hospitalised father before finally informing the president of the Security Council that "with a strong feeling of personal insufficiency, I hesitate to accept the candidature, but I do not feel that I could refuse the task imposed upon me".[11] Recommended by the Security Council, he was elected by the General Assembly at its 423rd plenary meeting on 7 April 1953 by secret ballot with 57 votes in favour, one against and one abstention. Upon arrival at Idlewild Airport in New York on 9 April, Hammarskjöld was greeted by his predecessor, welcoming him to "the most impossible job on this earth".[12]

Very soon, and much in contrast to his predecessor, Dag Hammarskjöld used his exceptional intellectual capacity and mind to elaborate in great detail his visions. As the four edited volumes of his public papers document, he frequently used forums outside the United Nations to present political-philosophical treatments of issues he felt a need to engage with. This included major speeches at internationally renowned universities, lengthy statements on other occasions when he was the invited guest speaker, as well as longer explanations at press conferences, which he had introduced as a regular form of exchange with representatives of the media. He also occasionally used debates in the General Assembly and the Security Council to explain his views and policies and outlined much of his vision in his introductions to the UN's annual reports. Taking such pronounced stands soon contradicted his initially declared personal dictum not to stand out. His typically *lagom* approach[13] was perhaps most poignantly articulated in a long interview published by the *New York Times* on 18 August 1953, in which he declared: "I am what I am. I am cast in a European mold of understatement. I do not wish to use, ever, one word that to my friends, or to myself, would sound false. A colorless sort of prophet, maybe."[14]

Talk about understatement! If anything, he was certainly not the "colourless sort of prophet", despite always being measured and self-controlled, at times bordering on introversion. His execution of duties soon demonstrated a degree of autonomy from the big powers, which they increasingly found a reason for concern. As we have seen, his election had been influenced by the assumption that he would be a low-profile technocrat, a "paper pusher" maybe, without vision or determination, a rather convenient recipient of instructions to be implemented without drama. As it turned out, this was a serious misjudgement.

His deep reflections provided a compass guiding his navigations through the contradictions of a global body in which fundamental differences between member states posed a constant challenge. Hammarskjöld responded by seeking to define the role of the United Nations and his own office in line with what he understood to be the substance and spirit of the Charter: "Instead of reading out bland equivocations written for him by staff, he used his speeches to articulate the public philosophy of an institution."[15] And he lived up to what he had written in his notebook in 1952: "Never, 'for the sake of peace and quiet', deny your own experience or conviction."[16]

Politics as Faith

Many of Hammarskjöld's views expressed on different occasions confirm that his job performance was much influenced by the ethics he had internalised during his upbringing and earlier career in the Swedish civil service.[17] They were rooted in his sense of duty as moulded in the tradition of Swedish society and reproduced for generations within his family. His public confession for a popular radio show at the beginning of his term in office left no doubt:

> The world in which I grew up was dominated by principles and ideals of a time far from ours and, as it may seem, far removed from the problems facing a man of the middle of the twentieth century. However, my way has not meant a departure from those ideals. On the contrary, I have been led to an understanding of their validity also for our world of today. Thus, a never abandoned effort frankly and squarely to build up a personal belief in the light of experience and honest thinking has led me to recognize and endorse, unreservedly, those very beliefs which once were handed down to me.

> From generations of soldiers and government officials on my father's side I inherited a belief that no life was more satisfactory than one of selfless service to your country—or humanity. This service required likewise the courage to stand up unflinchingly for your convictions.

> From scholars and clergymen on my mother's side I inherited a belief that, in the very radical sense of the Gospels, all men were equals as children of God, and should be met and treated by us as our masters in God.

Faith is a state of the mind and the soul. The language of religion is a set of formulas which register a basic spiritual experience. I was late in understanding what this meant. When I finally reached that point, the beliefs in which I was once brought up were recognized by me as mine in their own right and by my free choice. I feel that I can endorse those convictions without any compromise with the demands of that intellectual honesty which is the very key to maturity of mind.[18]

In his first end-of-year message, Hammarskjöld insisted that the private world within each individual must mark the beginning of any public work for peace:

To build for man a world without fear, *we* must be without fear. To build a world of justice, *we* must be just. And how can we fight for liberty if we are not free in our own minds? How can we ask others to sacrifice if *we* are not ready to do so? Some might consider this to be just another expression of noble principles, too far from the harsh realities of political life ... I disagree.[19]

Hammarskjöld's loyalty to ideals whose origins lay in earlier times manifested itself in a variety of convictions and principles, which reached far beyond the day-to-day execution of office. His sense of duty was an integral part of a wider conviction he also subsumed under faith. As "priest of a secular church",[20] he regarded the United Nations, while necessarily outside all confessions, as "an instrument of faith".[21] Based on his conviction that success would never be final but "found rather in the stamina to continue the struggle, and in the preservation and strengthening of faith in the future of man",[22] he stressed this core ethic of service numerous times during his early years in office:

It has rightly been said that the United Nations is what the Member nations make it. But it may likewise be said that, within the limits set by government action and government cooperation, much depends on what the Secretariat makes it. That is our pride in the Secretariat, and that is the challenge we have to face

...

The motto of one of the old ruling houses in Europe was: "I serve." This must be the guiding principle, and also the inspiration and the challenge, for all those who have to carry the responsibility of office for any community. Is it not natural that this motto should be felt with special faith, sincerity and loyalty by those who assist in the greatest venture in international cooperation on which mankind has ever embarked?[23]

Clearly influenced by his socialisation, Hammarskjöld summarised the "Uppsala tradition" as "a spiritual legacy beyond ... boundaries",[24] which he characterised positively as one with which he obviously identified:

At their best the representatives of this legacy show the quiet self-assurance of people firmly rooted in their own world, but they are, at the same time and for that very reason, able to accept and develop a true world citizenship. At the best they are not afraid to like the man in their enemy and they know that such liking gives an insight which is a source of strength. They have learned patience in dealings with mightier powers. They know that their only hope is that justice will prevail and for that reason they like to speak for justice. However, they also know the dangers and temptations of somebody speaking for justice without humility. They have learned that they can stand strong only if faithful to their own ideals, and they have shown the courage to follow the guidance of those ideals to ends which sometimes, temporarily, have been very bitter. And finally, the spirit is one of peace ...[25]

When addressing the Evanston Assembly of the World Council of Churches in 1954, he explained that for him the Charter of the United Nations

> referred to something which could be understood as God's will. By this he meant belief in the dignity and value of the individual and a shared desire to practise tolerance and live together in peace. For Hammarskjöld these propositions were analogous to the commandment to "love our neighbours as we love ourselves". While the UN necessarily stood outside of all confessions, the organization was nevertheless an instrument of faith as its aims were synonymous with God's will. Thus, despite their different functions, the UN and the churches stood side by side in the struggle to establish peace.[26]

For Hammarskjöld, who was sometimes called "a secular Pope",[27] the Charter was a kind of secular Bible.

> International law, as it is incarnated in the UN Charter, was for him the guiding light and source of inspiration, as well as the binding line of action, in everything he did ... he always returned to the idea of the particular importance of international law as a shield for the interests of small states against the arrogance of major powers and the pressure they might bring to bear. With great fervor he stood up for the primacy of law over power.[28]

He did so also for "selfish" reasons: "The UN Charter was more than a simple legal text for Hammarskjöld; it represented the foundational legitimation of his role and vocation."[29] His spiritual background did not prevent him from adopting a vision which shaped worldly norms and views as an integral part of the global contract that in his view was supposed to govern the United Nations.[30] He summed this up in the following words: "The United Nations is faith and works—faith in the possibility of a world without fear and works to bring that faith closer to realization in the life of men."[31] For him, shared values mattered. Serving the United Nations was in his eyes more than executing a job. Addressing the staff after his reappointment for a second term, he stated:

> We are not what we should be, we have not reached the full strength of our possible contribution, until we have managed to develop within ourselves, and in relations with others, the sense of belonging. We are no Vatican, we are no republic, we are not outside the world—we are very much in the world. But even within the world, there can be this kind of sense of belonging, this deeper sense of unity. I hope we are on the road to this sense.[32]

His "'visionary realism', for example his faith in human solidarity and reconciliation in times of 'planetary crisis'",[33] translated faith into politics just as politics were for him a matter of faith, as the Preamble of the Charter had stated: "to reaffirm faith in fundamental human rights, in the dignity and worth of the human person, in the equal rights of men and women and of nations large and small, and to establish conditions under which justice and respect for the obligations arising from treaties and other sources of international law can be maintained".

Solidarity and Universal Humanity

Hammarskjöld's engagement with others was guided by a deeply ingrained Swedish value system and identity in combination with a similarly deep religious spirituality. This, however, was not an ethnocentric limitation. It allowed him to expand the frontiers and the horizon with an open mind. It empowered him to engage with others, without fear or defensively, in the search for both commonalities among the human species and the variety of cultural, religious or other differences. Being a regular student of the classics of spirituality, including *The Imitation of Christ* by Thomas à Kempis[34] and the works of Meister Eckhart, and also familiar with the Buddhist tradition, Hammarskjöld was not confined to a certain theological or teleological mindset. He had an all-embracing approach towards humanity and human interaction in the spirit of mutual respect and the recognition of what in today's jargon would be termed "otherness". The ability to look outward from a firm inner world inspired one Swedish biographer to describe Hammarskjöld as "the first modern Swede".[35]

While speaking on "The World and the Nation" in mid-1955, he summed up the challenges of human emancipation in an era approaching the end of colonial rule:

> There is a new situation the day you have to recognize that you cannot dictate to other nations and that you are not independent of the actions of other nations. It

is more difficult to see your brother in a slave or a master. It is easier to see him in somebody with whom you have to live without giving or taking orders. Looking back into the past we see how peoples have been oppressed—and how peoples have accepted oppression—in the name of God. May we not be approaching a time when in His name they will instead be giving and accepting freedom?[36]

In one of his rare extemporaneous speeches, prompted by a moving encounter during a cultural event performed in his honour, Hammarskjöld addressed the Indian Council of World Affairs by stressing the universality of the human dimensions: "With respect to the United Nations as a symbol of faith, it may ... be said that to every man it stands as a kind of 'yes' to the ability of man to form his own destiny, and form his own destiny so as to create a world where dignity of man can come fully into its own."[37]

Another permanent feature of Hammarskjöld's thinking, related to the notion of solidarity, was the universal challenge of humanity, which knows no geographical limitations or restrictions of state borders but touches everyone. As he stated as early as 1954:

We know that the struggle for the souls of men between freedom and tyranny, between idealism and materialism, does not recognize national frontiers. Though one or the other may be dominant in a society at any one time, such dominance is a passing phenomenon. For the struggle belongs to all humanity and it is going on all the time in all societies of man. Thus the divisions that we see today between the nations should not be considered as fixed, or eternal, or even as basically significant in the geographical sense.[38]

This remained his credo years later:

The conflict between different approaches to the liberty of man and mind or between different views of human dignity and the right of the individual is continuous. The dividing line goes within ourselves, within our own peoples, and also within other nations. It does not coincide with any political or geographical boundaries. The ultimate fight is one between the human and the subhuman. We are on dangerous ground if we believe that any individual, any nation, or any ideology has a monopoly on rightness, liberty, and human dignity.[39]

He reiterated the same conviction upon return from a five-week tour through African countries when a journalist asked him "what the ideological trends are today in Africa, whether they stem from the inner realities facing African life today or whether they reflect the often repeated clichés of foreign ideology".[40] As he answered:

I do not think that the rights of man is a foreign ideology to any people and that, I think, is the key to the whole ideological structure in Africa at present. It may be that the most eloquent and the most revolutionary expressions of the rights of man are to be found in Western philosophers and Western thinking, but that certainly does not make the idea a Western idea imposed on anybody.[41]

One of Hammarskjöld's rare direct public comments on colonial rule was a speech at the University of Lund in 1959. Detecting a form of advancement "far beyond the world once mirrored by Kipling or Sven Hedin", he described nineteenth-century Europe as a

> tightly closed cultural world, highly developed but essentially regional in character.
>
> Goethe's "universality" was combined with a firm conviction of the supremacy of the European man of culture, a supremacy which erected invisible walls around his spiritual life in relation to other parts of the world ... Nobody should forget that colonization reflected a basic approach ... which often mirrored false claims, particularly when it touched on spiritual development. Applied generally, it was untenable.
>
> ...
>
> To a Westerner of a later generation who is facing today's Asia and Africa, it is a useful exercise to go back to the works written by distinguished Europeans whose mental attitude was shaped in the main before the First World War. What strikes one in the first place, perhaps, is how much they did *not* see and did *not* hear, and how even their most positive attempts at entering into a world of different thoughts and emotions were colored by an unthinking, self-assured superiority.[42]

Returning from a journey through several Asian countries in 1956, he pointed to the limited views of what later became known as Eurocentrism:

> We talk these days much about the Renaissance of Asia and the Asian peoples. We talk about a new nationalism, about the urge for independence and wider political influence for the peoples of Asia. I am afraid that in doing so we are sometimes so preoccupied with the specific problems and interests of what history calls 'the West' that we view these developments less in the light of what they contribute to the growth of all humanity than in the light of what they might detract from the predominance of Western peoples. We see what we may lose. We do not realize what we are gaining.[43]

Despite the absence of any postcolonial theory during those days, Hammarskjöld was aware that the "outer" colonialism was also a result of an "inner" colonialism, that of an internalised world. This was manifest in his insight that policy ultimately has a core in the inner nature of the individual actors involved and that it would be an error to believe that there is any "monopoly on rightness". On the occasion of the annual celebration of Human Rights Day on 10 December 1960, Hammarskjöld contemplated in a short statement the linkage between official policies and individual lack of emancipation, when he reminded his audience:

> The General Assembly is now engaged in a debate on the colonial issue. It is significant for the present international revolution. The progress toward self-determination and self-government for all peoples is truly an encouraging translation into political action of the concept of human rights and the underlying ethical ideas. But let us not forget that there is a colonialism of the heart and of the mind, which no political decision can overcome and against which the battle must be waged within ourselves, without any exception.[44]

He was keen not to lose sight of such an individual side to engagements with the outer world. Critical self-exploration and soul-searching was part of his approach to life: "The longest journey", he started one of his poems in his notebook in 1950, "is the journey inwards".[45] Decolonisation, one can infer from such insight, starts at home, both in the individual inner world and in the collective mindset of one's own society.

International Civil Service

Dag Hammarskjöld held a firm belief in the autonomy of the office of the Secretary-General and the Secretariat, which he felt ought not to be degraded to a mere instrument or conference machinery serving the interests of the powerful states. As has been said, the "discourse of international civil service and neutrality ... drew on the Secretary-General's main capital, namely the legal capital created by the UN Charter, which gave the Secretary-General a slim space of autonomy, primarily through Articles 99 and 100".[46] Hammarskjöld was determined not to surrender the power of definition to individual member states. Embedded in the ethic of the Swedish civil servant, he strongly advocated the autonomy of the staff serving at the United Nations, their loyalty to the Charter and other normative frameworks, but not to the country of their origin. "International service requires of all of us first and foremost the courage to be ourselves", he stated in the first of a series of pioneering speeches on the subject.[47] Already then, he summarised the fundamental challenge:

> If this is the essence of international service, such service will expose us to conflicts. It will not permit us to live lazily under the protection of inherited and conventional ideas. Intellectually and morally, international service therefore requires courage to admit that you, and those you represent, are wrong, when you find them to be wrong, even in the face of a weaker adversary, and courage to

defend what is your conviction even when you are facing the threats of powerful opponents. But while such an outlook exposes us to conflicts, it also provides us with a source of inner security; for it will give us "self-respect for our shelter".[48]

He dismissed the question whether such service "is possible without split loyalties in a divided world" as an unreal problem:

> We embrace ideals and interests in their own right, not because they are those of our environment or of this or that group. Our relations to our fellow men do not determine our attitude to ideals, but are determined by our ideals. If our attitude is consistent, we shall be consistent in our loyalties. If our attitude is confused, then our loyalties will also be divided.[49]

For him, the international civil servant "remains under the obligation that applies to all of us—to be faithful to truth as he understands it".[50] Faithfulness, faith, truth, loyalty and integrity are the keywords in his elaborations appealing to "the pursuit of happiness under the laws of conscience which alone can justify freedom".[51] Referring to Russell W. Davenport's *The Dignity of Man*, he concluded: "the dignity of man, as a justification for our faith in freedom, can be part of our living creed only if we revert to a view of life where maturity of mind counts for more than outward success and where happiness is no longer to be measured in quantitative terms".[52] Again he stressed the importance of "inner dialogue" as the source of one's values, with the results "evident as independence, courage, and fairness in dealing with others, evident in true international service".[53]

While the emphasis of this speech was on the conscience of individuals and the definition of their service, Hammarskjöld in a subsequent address shifted to the institutionalised structure of the international service by focusing on the mandate and role of the Secretariat, which for him was "a living thing", involving the convictions and hopes of its individual members and their idealisms, which he considered "independent of orders from any Government".[54] Based on his reading of the Charter, "the assistance that the Secretariat can give must be inspired only by the principles and aims of the Organization, independent of the special interests of any individual Members".[55] Such an understanding, which reflected the notion of the value-based autonomy of the individual international civil servant, entailed a crucial role and "heavy responsibility" for the Secretary-General in representing "the collective ideal". Being recognised through provisions in the Charter, it entitled him "to take initiatives in the Security Council when he considers that peace and security are seriously threatened".[56] He referred to Chapter XV of the Charter:

Article 99

The Secretary-General may bring to the attention of the Security Council any matter which in his opinion may threaten the maintenance of international peace and security.

Article 100

1. In the performance of their duties the Secretary-General and the staff shall not seek or receive instructions from any government or from any other authority external to the Organization. They shall refrain from any action which might reflect on their position as international officials responsibly only to the Organization.

He then added to the constitutional architecture of the United Nations the judicial aspect of international law, which in his view was left with "wide margins of uncertainty". He asked if it was "not in the interest of sound development to restrict as much as possible the arena where strength is an argument and to put as much as possible under the rule of law"—only to suggest that one should make "use of all possibilities to develop an international common law by submitting our conflicts to jurisdiction wherever that is possible".[57] He concluded that "the world of order and justice for which we are striving will never be ours unless we are willing to give it the broadest possible and the firmest possible foundation in law".[58] Through such explicit linkage, he combined his strong views on the independence of the international civil service with a similarly strong view on the constitutionally enshrined role of the Secretariat as a principal organ and the need for a binding legal international framework to enable the institution to operate as independently as possible from individual governments and states. But there seems to emerge an in-built tension between the moral conscience guiding the international civil service and international law "as the different bases of authority on which Hammarskjöld relied and his ability (and willingness) to shift between them in a pragmatic and flexible way".[59]

Here, the link between Hammarskjöld's intellectual background and his approach towards international law is instructive.[60] He adopted a "flexible" approach, which reconciled the recognition of global norms and principles with the application of ethical principles.[61] This is reflected in his contextual vision of norms and principles. As one of the early proponents of the link between peace, security and human rights, he perceived fundamental concepts, such as collective security or non-intervention, through the lens of human rights and human security, by focusing on "men" in addition to states, and on "dignity" in addition to security—a nexus that is recognised in United

Nations peace maintenance today. Hammarskjöld's personal ethics explain his openness towards Blue Helmet intervention and protection, as when the United Nations crossed the boundaries between peacekeeping and peace enforcement in the Congo. His approach towards law was based on the "natural law" understanding that written law needs to be reconciled "with a law of a higher order"—a position in line with his Christian values.[62]

During the United Nations intervention in the Congo from mid-1960 (dealt with in chapter six), all the principled values considered as the compass and coordinates for the international civil service were confronted with the ultimate test in practice. Soon the constraints showed the limitations of the theory. Having survived the attempt by the Soviet Union to oust him from office and to replace the office of the Secretary-General with a troika of representatives from the East, the West and the non-aligned countries, Hammarskjöld once again used a speech at a prominent institution of higher learning as his last resort to present his convictions. As his former legal advisor in the UN Secretariat observed twenty years after Hammarskjöld's death: "In its defense of personal integrity against the claims of power, and its invocation of reason and history, the lecture carries a powerful appeal even today."[63]

As his entry point, Hammarskjöld referred to a recent article by Walter Lippmann,[64] in which he quoted Khrushchev as having stated that "while there are neutral countries, there are no neutral men". Lippmann concluded that the view of the Soviet government was "that there can be no such things as an impartial civil servant in this deeply divided world, and that the kind of political celibacy which the British theory of the civil service calls for, is in international affairs a fiction".[65] Hammarskjöld then summarised the institutional development of the United Nations and its international civil service since the time of the League of Nations and its legacy in the Charter, stressing the notion of independence from national governments. Referring to Chapter XV ("The Secretariat") and its Articles 97 to 101, he explained why this allowed the "full political independence" of the Secretariat and gave the Secretary-General a mandate "with tasks involving the execution of political decisions [taken by the General Assembly or the Security Council], even when this would bring him—and with him the Secretariat and its members— into the arena of possible political conflict".[66] Based on his interpretation, he then concluded: "If a demand for neutrality is made, by present critics of the international civil service, with the intent that the international civil servant should not be permitted to take a stand on political issues, in response to requests of the General Assembly or the Security Council, then the demand is in conflict with the Charter itself."[67] He pointed to the fact that member states had on several occasions assigned the Secretary-General "functions which necessarily required him to take positions in highly controversial political matters", referring as the most prominent examples to Palestine and the Suez crisis in Egypt (both 1956), Lebanon (1958) and—the most recent and the one which had triggered the Soviet attacks on his office—the Republic of the Congo (1960).[68] He then concluded:

> the responsibilities of the Secretary-General under the Charter cannot be laid aside merely because the execution of decisions by him is likely to be politically controversial. The Secretary-General remains under the obligation to carry out the policies as adopted by the organs; the essential requirement is that he does this on the basis of his exclusively international responsibility and not in the interest of any particular state or groups of states.[69]

As he stressed at the end of his paradigmatic explanation:

> the international civil servant cannot be accused of lack of neutrality simply for taking a stand on a controversial issue when this is his duty and cannot be avoided. But there remains a serious intellectual and moral problem as we move within an area inside which personal judgment must come into play. Finally, we have to deal with the question of integrity or with, if you please, a question of conscience.

> The international civil servant must keep himself under the strictest observation. He is not requested to be a neuter in the sense that he has to have no sympathies or antipathies, that there are to be no interests which are close to him in his personal capacity or that he is to have no ideas or ideals that matter for him. However, he is requested to be fully aware of those human reactions and meticulously check himself so that they are not permitted to influence his actions. This is nothing unique. Is not every judge professionally under the same obligation?

> If the international civil servant knows himself to be free from such personal influence in his actions and guided solely by the common aims and rules laid down for, and by the Organization he serves and by recognized legal principles, then he has done his duty, and then he can face the criticism which, even so, will be unavoidable. As I said, at the last, this is a question of integrity, and if integrity in the sense of respect for law and respect for truth were to drive him into positions of conflict with this or that interest, then that conflict is a sign of his neutrality and not of his failure to observe neutrality—then it is in line, not in conflict with his duties as an international civil servant.[70]

Clearly, this passionate plea showed the traces which the ongoing conflict in the Congo, and not least the assassination of Lumumba, had left. Hammarskjöld's introduction to his annual report, written a month before his death, returned to the matter:

While it may be said that no man is neutral in the sense that he is without opinions or ideals, it is just as true that, in spite of this, a neutral Secretariat is possible. Anyone of integrity, not subjected to undue pressures, can regardless of his own views, readily act in an "exclusively international" spirit and can be guided in his actions on behalf of the Organization solely by its interests and principles, and by the instruction of its organs.[71]

Values vs Realpolitik

However, as compelling as these arguments might look at first sight, they seem to suggest an all-too-easy way out—especially for a person so driven by a fundamental belief as Dag Hammarskjöld was. His passionate advocacy of values was unable to eliminate the latent conflict between his own convictions and the mandate he had to execute, which was not completely of his own making. The interpretation of such a mandate leaves room for definition. And that room is occupied and claimed by a variety of potentially antagonistic stakeholders in global policy-making and their colliding interests. These include the values of the office-bearer, and also those of others with at times very different agendas and motives. Who then holds the power of definition? To resort, as Hammarskjöld occasionally did in such situations, to the ultimate dogma enshrined in the Charter did not really offer a way out of the dilemma. Rather, at times his appeals sounded more like appeals of ultimate desperation, for example when during the Suez crisis he stated before the Security Council in no uncertain terms:

> The principles of the Charter are, by far, greater than the Organization in which they are embodied, and the aims which they are to safeguard are holier than the policies of any single nation or people ... [T]he discretion and impartiality ... imposed on the Secretary-General ... may not degenerate into a policy of expediency. He must also be a servant of the principles of the Charter, and its aims must ultimately determine what for him is right or wrong.[72]

And in his introduction to the annual report for 1959–60 he confessed:

> It is my firm conviction that any result bought at the price of a compromise with the principles and ideals of the Organization, either by yielding to force, by disregard of justice, by neglect of common interests or by contempt for human rights, is bought at too high a price. That is so because a compromise with its principles and purposes weakens the Organization in a way representing a definite loss for the future that cannot be balanced by any immediate advantage achieved.[73]

And he reiterated that "an attempt to achieve results at the cost of principles is a loss not only for the future but also immediately in respect of the significance of the Organization on which its strength in our present-day world ultimately depends".[74]

At the beginning of his second term, after being reappointed without any opposing vote, he addressed a staff meeting by recalling his first appearance before this audience, outlining once again his credo:

> I felt that this kind of job—and it is true not only of my post but of very many of the jobs held here—is a job which carries with it very considerable risks. There is very much you can lose on them. But I knew one thing: that there is one thing that nobody needs to lose, and that is self-respect. And if I had any promise which I had in mind and which I gave to myself five years ago, it was just this one: Whatever happens, stick to your guns, so that you can feel satisfaction with what you have done, whatever the outcome.[75]

But how does "stick to your guns" translate into practice when executing a disputed mandate wide open to differing interpretations in a highly politicised environment, in which various parties watch each step taken with suspicion, guided by their own agendas? Hammarskjöld was particularly careful when it came to communication, an essential tool of mediation for ensuring trust and reliability. In late 1955 he wrote the following in his notebook:

> Respect for the word is the first commandment in the discipline by which a man can be educated to maturity—intellectual, emotional, and moral.
>
> Respect for the word—to employ it with scrupulous care and an incorruptible heartfelt love of truth—is essential if there is to be any growth in a society or in the human race.
>
> To misuse the word is to show contempt for man. It undermines the bridges and poisons the wells. It causes Man to regress down the long path of his evolution.[76]

For Hammarskjöld, being careful with words at times also meant using language deliberately as a tool for creating additional manoeuvring space. This can be seen in his complaints about the lack of clarity in Security Council resolutions for the Congo mission, while at the same time exploiting this lack of clarity:

> His interpretations of the already vague Council mandate were often couched in language which meant different things to different people. This was not duplicity on his part. He regarded such abstruseness as essential to give him sufficient latitude to act effectively when there was agreement only that something should be done. The British and French criticized him for this quality. A French representative once called him a "master of the calculated imprecision".[77]

He thus made use of the margin of interpretation provided by any ambiguity in these resolutions; as Conor Cruise O'Brien observed, through "ambiguities resolved, through margins skilfully used, the office of Secretary-General had grown in stature and authority far beyond what the framers of the Charter seem to have envisaged at San Francisco".[78] That language indeed mattered a lot in Hammarskjöld's diplomacy and negotiation style can be illustrated by the following episode, narrated by a young translator working from 1959 in the office of the Secretary-General. As he recalled:

> Dag Hammarskjöld attended personally to every detail. He once called me early in the morning. I had just arrived at the office and felt honoured to receive a call from the Secretary-General. Actually he went straight to the point and explained the reason for his call:
>
> "Did you edit the French version of the resolution that was distributed this morning?"
>
> "Yes, Mr. Secretary-General."
>
> "But you changed the text of operative paragraph 2. Why?"
>
> "Yes indeed. The text was submitted in English and in the original language that paragraph had two possible meanings. In order to avoid any ambiguity in French, a precise language, I thought it was my duty to select the only plausible version."
>
> "That is exactly what you shouldn't have done. The final text was the result of a compromise. Please issue a revised document that restores the original text."
>
> As I immediately complied with the Secretary-General's instructions, I realized that in spite of the Cold War, a draft resolution did not have to be voted upon in its original form but could be negotiated with a view to reaching a consensus. It was really the beginning of a new trend which is now an established practice.[79]

Hammarskjöld also introduced and used press conferences as a means to convey messages. According to Brian Urquhart, these "were often a masterpiece of elliptical statements, circumlocutions and elegant dodging of questions, although when the occasion required he spoke his mind with the greatest clarity. Being hard to get and even harder to pin down was an important asset in preserving the interest of the media and the public."[80] As Urquhart summed it up elsewhere, his regular interactions with the press corps were "a masterly mixture of abstraction, reflection and a minimum of hard news".[81]

In a press conference less than two weeks after his famous speech at Oxford, the journalists present revisited the role of his office. Confronted with the assumption "that objectivity or neutrality is irreconcilable with the working of the human mind and that there is not a single neutral person on this globe", Hammarskjöld responded:

It may be true that in a very deep, human sense there is no neutral individual, because, as I said in Oxford, everyone, if he is worth anything, has to have his ideas and ideals—things which are dear to him, and so on. But what I do claim is that even a man who is in that sense not neutral can very well undertake and carry through neutral actions, because that is an act of integrity ... I am not neutral as regards the Charter; I am not neutral as regards facts. But that is not what we mean. What is meant by "neutrality" in this kind of debate is, of course, neutrality in relation to interests: and there I do claim that there is no insurmountable difficulty for anybody with the proper kind of guiding principles in carrying through such neutrality one hundred percent.[82]

But even Dag Hammarskjöld showed signs of wear and tear. At the beginning of his second term in office he had still expressed a "belief and the faith that the future will be all right because there will always be enough people to fight for a decent future".[83] But in mid-June 1961, his friend Bo Beskow asked him—as he usually did when they met—if he still had faith in the individual. While previously the answer had always been positive, he now responded: "No I never thought it possible, but lately I have come to understand that there are really evil persons—evil right through—only evil."[84] A few months earlier he had observed in a letter to a friend: "The Congo crisis continues its wild course of events, with frightening elements of irresponsibility, intrigues, untruthfulness and cruelty. This really is a history that soon must be written, written by a cold head and a sharp pen, as a frightening picture of our world and of our present-day humanity."[85]

A closer look, in the midst of such "frightening elements", suggests that even the essentially optimistic "Hammarskjöld approach" was in practice much more sober and pragmatic than his principled statements seem to suggest. His "approach to the UN and international law was not to rely on drawn out political compromise but on *ad hoc* arrangements responding to urgent and concrete needs".[86] While the postulates linking law, morality and expertise, looked at separately, seem convincing in their own right, their reconciliation—especially in a context where the interest and influence of powerful member states directly affected the decision-making process within the United Nations—seems more wishful thinking than a realistic agenda. After all,

> law intersects and interacts, in a myriad ways, with two other modes of discourse and practice: value-rational and affective frameworks motivated by the concerns of morality, and the instrumental rationality of different forms of expertise. Thus, the everyday work of international civil servants requires them not only to deal in the currency of legal arguments and instruments but also to draw upon

moral purposes and technical means that are present in their institutional settings as well as their own personal values and professional training.[87]

On 8 September 1961, Hammarskjöld addressed the staff at the Secretariat in New York before his departure to the Congo. It turned out to be the last time. His words spoken then sound like a legacy:

> What is at stake is a basic question of principle: Is the Secretariat to develop as an international secretariat, with the full independence contemplated in Article 100 of the Charter, or is it to be looked upon as an intergovernmental—not international—secretariat providing merely the necessary administrative services for a conference machinery? This is a basic question, and the answer to it affects not only the working of the Secretariat but the whole of the future of international relations ... There is only one answer to the human problem involved, and that is for all to maintain their professional pride, their sense of purpose, and their confidence in the higher destiny of the Organization itself, by keeping to the highest standards of personal integrity in their conduct as international civil servants and in the quality of the work that they turn out on behalf of the Organization. This is the way to defend what they believe in and to strengthen this Organization as an instrument of peace for which they wish to work ... It is false pride to register and to boast to the world about the importance of one's work, but it is false humility, and finally just as destructive, not to recognize—and recognize with gratitude—that one's work has a sense. Let us avoid the second fallacy as carefully as the first, and let us work in the conviction that our work *has* a meaning beyond the narrow individual one and *has* meant something for man.[88]

In 1952, before knowing that he would become the world's highest international civil servant, he had written in his notebook: "Never, 'for the sake of peace and quiet', deny your own experience or convictions."[89] Four years later he ended a speech in his office with the words: "It is when we all play safe that we create a world of the utmost insecurity. It is when we all play safe that fatality will lead us to our doom. It is 'in the dark shade of courage' alone that the spell can be broken."[90]

5

DAG HAMMARSKJÖLD, THE COLD WAR, DEVELOPMENT AND AFRICA

I am convinced that the United Nations cannot render its new African Member states and the whole community of nations in Africa a greater service than to assist them, within the framework of their own efforts, to mould their new national and regional life, now that they enter the community of nations, in ways that will give Africa its rightful place on the international scene.[1]

Hammarskjöld's predecessor, Trygve Lie, could to some extent be regarded as the first victim of "collateral damage" on the stage of global governance, when the interests of the Soviet Union clashed with those of the Western states. As we have seen, Hammarskjöld, the "unknown Swede", was considered a suitable replacement by the Security Council's permanent members, because he was perceived as a bureaucratic administrator. This suited the interests of those who preferred to set the agenda in global governance largely undisturbed by any difficult official, who might even have his own ideas of how to "run the show".

Trying to act in a non-partisan way, loyal to the values and principles of the United Nations Charter, while carrying out often vague resolutions wide open to different interpretations, Hammarskjöld was at times caught between a rock and a hard place. The following example illustrates his difficulty in navigating a course between the Soviet Union and the United States:

> when the Soviet Union announced its policy of unilateral cessation of nuclear tests in April 1958, Mr. Hammarskjold "welcomed" this step. (Some United

States officials considered his remark somewhat out of character with his role.) Three weeks later, Mr. Hammarskjold "welcomed" the initiative taken by the United States in presenting a proposal for aerial inspections of the Arctic. (Soviet representatives considered his remark somewhat out of character with his role.)[2]

While the nuclear arms race and disarmament were a major focus in the East–West rivalries and in Hammarskjöld's negotiations,[3] geographical territories under the influence or control of the dominant states also provided an ongoing source of conflict. Hammarskjöld on several occasions was painfully reminded of the limits of his office. From Guatemala to Hungary and from Laos to Bizerte, to mention only a few prominent cases,[4] the influence of the big powers and the exercise of their veto rights in the Security Council were already able to prevent any meaningful role by the United Nations in conflict intervention against their will.

The Cold War era was of course by no means limited to disputes in the sphere of diplomacy. Evidence now available suggests that the superpower rivalry was a fertile ground for all sorts of violations of fundamental principles of peaceful interaction, including invasion of countries and the killing of those individuals considered to be in the way of the great powers' geostrategic interests. Cold War antagonisms were not a kindergarten game.[5] One should nevertheless refrain from foregone conclusions and from abandoning the solid ground of trustworthy interpretation based on reliable and verified facts. But it is difficult to ignore the indications that something was deeply rotten in the state of world affairs—then as much as today. Showdowns such as deliberately planned assassinations and coups, however, remained until 1960 mainly matters that happened outside Africa.

Africa and the Cold War

As surprising as this might sound, few of the Cold War-motivated animosities and interventions played out during the 1950s on the African continent. It only became a battlefield of big power competition and rivalry starting with events unfolding in the Congo from mid-1960 onward. Political contestation was certainly influenced, at least indirectly, also by external interests apart from those of the colonial powers and affected the agenda in many of the decolonisation processes from the mid-1950s. Control over strategic resources was also a factor in rivalries and dubious practices by all sorts of unsavoury elements, even as part of the competition within the Western alliance of states, as the example of the uranium deposits at the Shinkolobwe mine in Katanga shows.[6] But these rivalries had only a limited impact on local political contexts, since "neither superpower spent much time thinking about Africa".[7]

This suited Hammarskjöld, who "fostered a particular vision of the UN as an activist and interventionist organisation which should prevent the spread of the Cold War to the newly independent African and Asian nations, by providing them with a safe haven which would guarantee their sovereignty".[8] Expectations that the governments of new member states, often emerging from a struggle for self-determination in anti-colonial movements, would use their growing influence in the bodies of the world organisation were often disappointed. They tended to display a "limited range of concerns" and "became almost exclusively devoted to the issues of decolonization, the human rights of nonwhite [sic] peoples, and economic and social progress and aid", while having "much less interest in East–West issues … or matters of international law."[9]

The Cold War rivalry entered African territory for the first time in January 1956 in a rather benign way, when a Soviet delegation attended the inauguration of President William Tubman in Liberia.[10] Pauline Frederick, the first US woman to report from and within the United Nations, observed in the same year, 1956, that the United Nations had become "an extension of the State Department dedicated to repelling Communist diplomacy".[11] In her view, decolonisation during the 1950s fuelled the Cold War, while Hammarskjöld considered the United Nations more "as an agency whose main function of representing the world's most powerful nations had begun to shift to one that would eventually be composed primarily of the world's smaller, emerging nations".[12]

From his early days in office, Hammarskjöld indeed paid much attention to those at the margins of global power structures—not to keep them there, but to find ways of assisting them through economic and social policies as a way of stabilising their governance.

> Hammarskjöld clearly realised that if the United Nations was to survive as the unique instrument for peaceful solution of conflicts that it was intended to be, there was an urgent need for a shift of emphasis from the purpose of preserving the established international order—or disorder—of the Cold War period to the purpose of meeting and dealing in a constructive way with the new challenges represented by the developing countries in Africa and Asia".[13]

That he did not succeed is another matter—and it also does not mean that he did not try.

Decolonisation and Development

As a trained economist who had been instrumental in the architecture of the social welfare state in Sweden during the 1930s and 1940s, Dag Hammarskjöld devoted much time to promoting matters of economic development and social justice. Just three months after his appointment, he presented for the first time the (eighth) annual report to the United Nations member states. Like his predecessor, Trygve Lie, he used the opportunity of an introduction to present his major annual policy statement and review. After a long general assessment, outlining his understanding of the organisation and the international civil service, he devoted attention to three aspects under the headings "Collective Security and Reconciliation", "Economic Development" and "Programme for Social Advancement and Human Rights". Notably, his thoughts on economic development occupied more room than the other two aspects together. Even at that stage he emphasised the role of the United Nations in linking economics, sovereignty and international collaboration by recognising

> the vital importance, for sound development of the world community, of orderly progress of the nations towards a state of full economic development, self-government, and independence. And, finally, international cooperation is recognized as an essential instrument for a guided development towards greater social justice within the nations.
>
> ...
>
> Of the multitude of United Nations programmes in the economic and social field in which the governments of Members have joined their efforts for their common benefit, none is more significant or less costly in the building of a better world community than the sharing of skills now universally known as technical assistance.[14]

His views were inspired by the experiences of the United Nations Technical Assistance Administration (TAA), established in 1950 with the Canadian diplomat Hugh Llewellyn Keenleyside as its Director-General. During its years in existence, it had a staff of almost 200, with more than 600 experts from 55 countries, serving in 65 other countries. Despite objections from Great Britain, France and the US (which was the main contributor to its budget), "Keenleyside worked to overcome Soviet suspicion of UN technical assistance work, ultimately bringing the Soviet Union and its allies into the work program".[15] The TAA played a crucial role in positioning the United Nations "as a primary actor in global economics and to enhance the aspirations of developing countries".[16] It "had a clear vision, emphasizing helping

'Third World' countries to write and implement national development plans inspired by left-leaning European Social Democratic governments".[17] Hammarskjöld was certainly close to this approach, which was advocated by leading economists operating from within the United Nations system, such as Gunnar Myrdal,[18] Hans Singer[19] and Raúl Prebisch.[20]

His personal interest in economic affairs motivated his active participation in the sessions of the Economic and Social Council (ECOSOC), which he attended repeatedly. At its meetings during the first half of July 1954 in Geneva, he delivered in total four statements. His views were also included in the introduction to his next annual report. It again recognised the "Tasks in the Field of Economic Policy" in a separate part, in which he expressed special concern over "the relationship of prices of raw materials with those of manufactured commodities".[21] While he stressed that the organisation "cannot, and should not, interfere with, or exert pressure on, domestic policies", he suggested that "it can assist ... by providing careful analyses of the problems involved and guidance as to the international economic framework within which such policies have to be pursued".[22] He alerted members "to the singular importance of the technical assistance programmes, so far the most successful experiment in channelling 'know how' and experience to those countries which have lagged behind in general technical and administrative development".[23]

While he was originally considered close to the school of thought inspired by John Maynard Keynes, Hammarskjöld differed from the policies advocated by the progressive economists in the United Nations agencies, who stressed full employment as a priority. Emerging as recommended strategy within regional bodies in the late 1940s, these approaches were criticised and rejected by the most influential Western states as "extreme Keynesianism". In the controversies he entered during his early years in office, Hammarskjöld distanced himself from these recommendations. After the 1954 ECOSOC meeting, he informed Gunnar Myrdal in a confidential letter that he shared his frustration with the undue political interference of the US delegates during the deliberations, exceeding by far their mandate as bureaucrats. But he dismissed Myrdal's approach given the need "to proceed with caution—also in relation to the friendliest governments—in my efforts to widen and consolidate recognized rights".[24] By retreating from "'extreme Keynesianism', Hammarskjöld steered the UN onto the less divisive ground of economic development."[25] His move has been interpreted as a pragmatic position in a geopolitical context: "The issue was obviously popular with developing countries, while both the East and the West could embrace it since in the context of the Cold War both stood to gain from giving aid to developing countries."[26]

When he again participated in the annual ECOSOC debate in Geneva in 1955, he advocated "creating a spirit of dynamic entrepreneurship, private and public, in areas where it is non-existent, for introducing modern technology and economic, social, and political institutions appropriate to a market economy".[27] In a journal article published in mid-1955, he stressed that "the machinery of the United Nations and its related agencies" should play a role in formulating and putting into effect long-term policies "for assisting the economically underdeveloped areas of the world to reach a level of economic and social development which will permit them to take their proper place in the world community".[28] Technical assistance programmes should be a collective task as an investment in peace, acknowledging that recipients "prefer in general to receive it from international sources rather than from any individual country".[29] Such machinery, he added, "may also be used to provide a means for the development, in peace, towards self-determination and independence of those non-self-governing peoples reaching political maturity".[30]

On a visit to India in February 1956, he once again emphasised the central importance of United Nations support for global economic development:

> I would say that the main trouble with the Economic and Social Council at present is that, in public opinion and in practice, the Council has not been given the place it should have in the hierarchy of the main organs of the United Nations ... Economic and social problems should rank equal with political problems. In fact, sometimes I feel that they should, if anything, have priority. While the Security Council exists primarily for settling conflicts which have arisen, the Economic and Social Council exists primarily to eliminate the causes of conflicts by working to change those conditions in which the emotional, economic, and social background for conflicts develops. The Economic and Social Council has a basic responsibility, and this basic responsibility should be recognized in its position and in the respect it enjoys.[31]

Submitting a paper for the annual ECOSOC debate in July 1956, he pointed to the flaws in the international commodity markets. He bemoaned "the absence of a framework of international policy", which left the underdeveloped countries on their own. Referring to critical judgements of their economic policies as "contrary to the letter and spirit of the Bretton Woods agreements", he asked: "how many of those who belabour the underdeveloped countries in this fashion have given adequate thought to the structure of world economic relationships which has forced these countries into unorthodox patterns of behaviour?"[32]

Giving preference to bilateral rather than multilateral aid "was a source of constant irritation to Hammarskjöld, since he believed that technical assistance was best provided in an integrated, not piecemeal, fashion". He was of the strong conviction that "only the United Nations could successfully remove technical assistance from the influence of bilateral or Cold War politics".[33] As Brian Urquhart maintains: "Hammarskjold's deep sense of the inequality of nations, in terms of both opportunity and of actual position, led him to believe that some form of international social consciousness should be fostered through a well-equipped and powerful system of international organizations."[34] Originally involved as a Swedish official in the establishment of the Committee of European Economic Co-operation, he was indignant about its transformation into the OECD, which then concerned itself with issues of development in the so-called Third World countries: "He regarded this change as the intrusion of a rich man's club into problems that were within the rightful jurisdiction of the more democratic and broadly based United Nations."[35] When in mid-December 1960 Hammarskjöld learned that the OECD planned to make a US$60 million grant to the Mobutu regime in the Congo, his unpublished communication to the United States and Great Britain expressed concern that this could be seen as interference by European colonial powers (including Belgium). He warned that this might "easily give rise to a situation in which the United Nations civilian operation in the fields of finance and trade should be discontinued".[36] In contrast, and despite its limited material resources, the architecture for technical assistance emerging during the 1950s within the United Nations system had involved a significant shift: "It was no small achievement to establish norms that emphasized the sovereignty of the recipient government and its primacy within a policy area where power relations among the parties have been characterized by extreme asymmetry."[37]

Enter(ing) Africa

As the number of Asian countries joining the member states in the United Nations grew from the late 1940s, decolonisation and development entered the agenda of global governance. As we have seen, the Bandung Conference of 1955 marked a turning point in the efforts of these states to act and speak together. Dag Hammarskjöld soon afterwards expressed words of recognition—if not appreciation—while on a visit to India:

> A year ago there was a significant conference in Bandung. Some people looked
> upon it as a warning—or even as a threat—from the United Nations angle. I

confess that I saw it never in that way, and I must say that the results of the conference, as expressed in its decisions and resolutions, with their strong emphasis on adherence to the principles of the United Nations Charter, confirmed those who felt that this was a sound and natural development which, in its final results, should strengthen the process of international cooperation embodied in the United Nations.[38]

Limited technical assistance by the TAA during the 1950s was largely offered to states in Asia, the Middle East and South America, one significant exception being Guinea.

It was the only colony that did not ratify the new Constitution of France (1958), since this document did not unambiguously endorse the right of African countries to independence. In consequence, France withdrew all its financial and technical support from the country. Hammarskjöld stepped in to help Guinea, at the cost of much resentment from President Charles de Gaulle. The UN took the unusual step of sending in a representative to help the country manage its independence and obtain assistance from other sources. Hammarskjöld also made clear that the country had to make its own policy decisions based on an assessment of local conditions. Thus when Sékou Touré, the Guinean leader, asked Hammarskjöld for advice on economic policies, Hammarskjöld replied that such decisions should be made by the country itself.[39]

From 1960 Hammarskjöld's more general statements on decolonisation, which until then mainly referred to the newly independent countries in Asia, saw a more pronounced inclusion of the newly independent or soon-to-be independent African countries. Aware of the new dynamics unfolding on the continent, Hammarskjöld left on 22 December 1959 for a five-week journey through twenty-one African countries.[40] During and after the trip he made some significant statements, which to a large extent related to matters of capacity-building during the initial stages of independence, when the colonial administration was replaced by a local government. While in Dar es Salaam, a journalist wanted to know if, in the case of a lack of administrative capacity in Tanganyika, the United Nations would be able to assist. Hammarskjöld expressed the concern that filling gaps with international civil servants rather than from national cadres risked turning such an administration into a new international bureaucracy. Referring to technical assistance by the TAA, he explained that "within strict limits and for specific tasks" experts would be recruited, provided that it was "on the initiative and at the request of the government". Furthermore, a major part of the expert's duty would be to train someone local as a replacement, "to render himself unnecessary".[41] Four days later, in extemporaneous remarks at the University Institute of Somalia, he stressed the need to accept the challenge which decades later found its expression in the slogan "African solutions to African problems", namely

> to create an international world, a world of universality and unity, and on the other hand to save not only what I would like to call the personality of Africa, but the personality of each country, each group, in this wonderfully rich continent. ... What is needed is unity with diversity, diversity respected within the framework of an even deeper respect for unity.[42]

Attending the second session of the Economic Commission for Africa, he returned to a theme he had already elaborated in a speech to students at Lund University:

> Partnership and solidarity are the foundations of the United Nations and it is in order to translate these principles into practical measures of economic cooperation that we are gathered today in this hall ... The emergence of Africa on the world scene, more than any other single phenomenon, has forced us to reappraise and rethink the nature of relationships among peoples at different stages of development, and the conditions of a new synthesis making room for an accelerated growth and development of Africa.[43]

He then continued at great length to set out his views on what may have been his most programmatic vision, observing that "the process of speedy emancipation is now, to a significant extent, being carried out in a manner which is consonant with the principles of the Charter". The United Nations, he continued, participated in this process "in order to make this momentous transition as peaceful and as humanitarian as possible, not only in political, but also in social and economic terms".[44] He then indicated his awareness of the fundamental decisions to be taken and their long-term implications, "which will, for many years to come, determine the patterns of their national life, as well as their relationships with the rest of the world". These included "difficult problems of monetary and currency systems", the orientation of trade relationships and defining "the role and magnitude of the public sector, and the system of property relationships". Such momentous and not easily reversible decisions "have to be made at a time when a country may lack a precise notion of its own identity in economic and financial terms, when it has had no time to draw a balance sheet of its assets and liabilities, which sometimes are inextricably entangled in those of another country or of a larger economic area, and when it has not been able to get a clearer picture of its own resources and needs". As he added, governments would have to make such fundamental decisions for themselves, "for which outside *expertise* cannot be of great assistance".[45]

Upon his return to New York, Hammarskjöld offered further insights into his approach at a press conference, where he stressed "the necessity of moral support" as "the most significant, because people and money and education do not mean a thing unless they are given and provided in the right spirit". This should manifest in "a sympathetic understanding, neither a feeling of false superiority, nor a feeling of sterile pessimism, nor a feeling of facile optimism"—but rather some degree of realism through support "provided by all the member states of the United Nations and by the Organization itself, which has pledged itself to self-government and to independence as part of the human rights spelled out in the Charter".[46] He then concluded by expressing preference for the provision of support through an international body of which the recipients were members.

> It is not until and unless the receiving country feels that this is an act of solidarity within an organization where they have equal rights with the donors that you really reach the optimum point not only psychologically but politically and economically.

> Under such circumstances, you are not surprised to hear that every place there was one wish reiterated—that as much as possible of international assistance should be channelled through the United Nations.[47]

When towards the end of the press conference he was asked about his views on the nature of economic aid to newly independent countries, Hammarskjöld replied that he had no views as to the forms of support: "They must grow organically out of their own thinking and their own problems."[48]

As a follow-up to two resolutions on economic and technical assistance to former trust territories and other newly independent states by the General Assembly during its session in 1959, Hammarskjöld submitted a memorandum to ECOSOC in April 1960. He emphasised again the need for assistance "which does not carry overtones or give rise to any discussions which might complicate the domestic policies and the effort to establish a firm domestic administration". The United Nations should act "as a kind of stopgap organization ... during those days when assistance is a necessity". Such assistance should provide "a little bit of elbow room ... during the first period" of independence.[49] It "should be very much in the hands, or entirely in the hands, of the governments concerned to decide how best to act and where best to act".[50]

While he was occupied from mid-1960 with the emerging crisis in the Congo, Hammarskjöld spent much time on his introduction to the annual report, giving "attention, in the first place, to the problem of Africa and its importance for the international community".[51] Commenting on the rapid increase of independent states joining the United Nations, he stated: "The African developments are putting the United Nations to a test as regards the functions of its parliamentary institutions and as regards the efficiency and strength of its executive capacity".[52] And he concluded:

> It is my firm conviction that the addition of a great number of new Member States will widen the perspectives, enrich the debate and bring the United Nations closer to present-day realities. I also believe that this development will exercise a sound influence in the direction of a democratization of proceedings by lessening the influence of firm groupings with firm engagements.[53]

But the support by the "established" and better-off member states of such an active role of the organisation as a kind of "midwife" enhancing post-colonial governance was in material terms as modest as its impact. A recent assessment clearly shows the limitations to the implementation of Hammarskjöld's ambitions and visions regarding the role of the United Nations in this sphere:

> Run with a skeletal staff by UN Secretariat officials and the modest amount of US$250,000 from the regular UN budget, OPEX [the UN programme to provide operational and executive personnel] had a slow start in 1959. That first year, only ten UN officials were dispatched under the programme. Among them were a director of broadcasting in Jamaica, a general manager at the Nepal Bank in Kathmandu, an air traffic controller in Tunisia, a director for the National Centre for Administrative Studies in Laos, and an administrative director at the Finance Ministry in Panama. Increasing demands for OPEX-type assistance convinced a majority of governments to end the initial "experimental period" the following year and put the scheme on a continuing basis in 1960. The same year, sixteen new African member states were admitted to the UN, yet only nineteen appointments were made through the OPEX programme. This hardly constituted the world-scale response to decolonization that Hammarskjöld had originally envisaged.[54]

In the introduction to his last annual report, Hammarskjöld—four weeks before his death—returned to his idea of the role of the Secretariat as regards technical assistance, now that the TAA had been transformed into OPEX in his office. As he noted, the initiative had so far "been less influenced by the conflict between different concepts of the role of the Organization than its activities in other fields".[55] He ended by reiterating what he considered the ultimate guiding principle of such involvement:

> Basic to the United Nations approach to economic and technical assistance is the principle under all circumstances that, although the Organization has to follow its own rules and maintain its own independence, its services are exclusively designed to meet the wishes of the recipient government, without the

possibility of any ulterior motives and free from the risk of any possible influence on the national or international policies of that government. Whatever development the executive activities of the Organization may show in the field, there should never be any suspicion that the world community would wish or, indeed, could ever wish to maintain for itself, through the United Nations, a position of power or control in a member country.[56]

He hereby repeated what he had already stressed in his introduction to the annual report in the previous year in the context of the "winds of change" and the conflict in the Congo:

The Organization must further and support policies aiming at independence, not only in the constitutional sense of the word, protecting the possibilities of the African peoples to choose their own way without undue influences being exercised and without attempts to abuse the situation. This must be true in all fields—the political, the economic, as well as the ideological—if independence is to have a real meaning.

...

If the Organization is willing and able to face its duties, it will have given the new nations of Africa the framework of which they are in need during the first and sensitive years of independence. It will also be helping the African world, in solidarity, to determine its own political personality in the setting of universality as represented by the United Nations.[57]

Throughout his terms in office, Hammarskjöld remained closely involved in matters of assistance to those states that joined the United Nations after decolonisation and looked for ways how best the organisation could support them. This included the conviction that they should be given a voice in international monetary matters and the global financial institutions.

He was the only Secretary-General ever to be invited to speak (and yet only once) at the annual meeting of the IMF and the World Bank. He never quite accepted the idea that the United Nations Organization should be debarred from discussing these matters and from seeking to influence them even if it could not hope to assume operational responsibilities for them.[58]

As the UN Under-Secretary-General in charge of Economic and Social Affairs recalled, Hammarskjöld told him in their last exchange before his untimely death, "in a half-serious, half-jocular mood: 'Before you and I depart from the scene we must do something with *that* ECOSOC.'"[59]

The Limits to Independence and Development

As the modest performance of OPEX illustrated, powerful member states, despite lacking fundamental objectives to the declared aims, were anything but supportive of the central role of the Secretariat envisaged by Hammarskjöld. With limited resources allocated after years of deliberation, it was hardly able to offer meaningful expertise and training. In contrast to such "soft support" in strengthening capacity in governance and administrative functions, the "hard core" macroeconomic matters such as international trade management, "capital transfer and financial stability were entrusted to organisations outside the UN system proper, with voting and decision-making structures controlled to a greater extent by richer countries—such as the General Agreement on Tariffs and Trade (GATT), the World Bank and the International Monetary Fund (IMF)".[60] Little seems to have changed since then, except for a new role for the organisation's agencies in humanitarian crises.

Looking back, not many of the hopes for self-reliant economic transformation towards more socially just societies were realised in the independent states on the African continent. The approach promoted by Hammarskjöld remained largely ineffective and bordered on wishful thinking. But despite the little impact it seems to have had, his approach has since then been the subject of harsh criticism. At times it seems as if Hammarskjöld is in retrospect given sole responsibility for the continuing asymmetries and inequalities that exist in the world today, for example when it is maintained that the economic thinking he advocated and applied in the process of decolonisation had "tragic consequences".[61] This perspective argues that his position was based on "the need for executive intervention to maintain order, and the commitment to government neutrality ... aimed at maintaining order and protecting life until what he called the 'political vacuums' caused by decolonisation could be filled".[62] Such an approach, described as neoliberalism, gave preference—so it is claimed—to stability over freedom by limiting the state to an agency with executive authority and leaving the economy to the free market. But Hammarskjöld's doctrine of strict neutrality only applied to the role of the United Nations. The new governments had of course not only the freedom but the responsibility to make policy choices. Linking in this context Hammarskjöld's economic thinking to the particular case of the Congo does not strengthen the criticism but rather blurs the lines of argument even further. It suggests that the role of the United Nations Secretariat in the conflict situation in the Congo was guided by some rigorous economic fundamentalism instead of reacting to and being dependent upon the much wider geostrategic constellation of forces represented in the Security Council and the General Assembly, which imposed limitations on the UN's mandate that were certainly as much political as anything else. The critical narrative shifts, not by coincidence but out of necessity, towards the way the political situation was handled—only to apportion ultimate responsibility for what happened on the ground to Hammarskjöld's economic thinking developed during the building of the Swedish welfare state:

> From his reorganisation of the Secretariat through to the conduct of the UN operation in the Congo, Hammarskjöld treated the commitment to neutrality as a core requirement both of the office of the Secretary-General and of the Secretariat. While neutrality is often interpreted as a political concept, it is useful to remember that economics was the mode of politics in which Hammarskjöld's thinking about neutrality, as well as his belief in the necessity of executive rule, had been shaped.[63]

Such reasoning ignores the numerous important interpretations offered by Hammarskjöld of the Charter, of other normative frameworks and the role of the international civil servant, which are anything but an economistically reductive vision. One can certainly see in his later career the influence of the Swedish civil servant, who expanded his concept of duty in the service of a caring state when he became Secretary-General serving the United Nations and its Charter. But this was a much more principled conviction than that of an economist, and his economic thinking was far from being his guiding compass. To that extent, the criticism seems rather conveniently constructed to apportion blame and might have been more convincing if more nuanced. In such criticism, Hammarskjöld's ideas of economic development based on technical assistance are given too much prominence as a determining factor if one considers the overall context of the global architecture and the structural determinants of those days. After all, his ideas were only implemented on a very limited scale with hardly any larger impact, given the reluctance of the big member states to replace bilateral mechanisms of influence by multilateral ones. As a review essay has remarked: "even granting that Hammarskjöld might have held views that aligned with neoliberal economic theories, more evidence would be needed to show that these views were actually implemented to a significant extent in the practice of the UN and other specialized agencies and that they were more determinative of outcomes than, say, the actions of powerful states, the initiatives of local actors and non-aligned states or private business interests".[64]

Another criticism that deserves rebuttal overly simplifies matters through selectivity. Its point of departure is the claim that the United Nations served to "anchor the new states firmly within the capitalist world" and that "Hammarskjöld's international administrative service shows how UN officials actively supported the dismantling of formal empires" in direct competition with the colonial powers. The "officially apolitical international civil servants" acted "in the Cold War battle for the development of the so-called Third World" in the hope that the countries would use their "elbow room" to "become more like 'the West'".[65] Evidence offered for this conclusion is a speech by Hammarskjöld on the international administrative service and subsequent press conference, held on 30 May 1956 at McGill University. It is, however, instructive to compare the quotations used with the full document.

The main quote has several omissions. This does not distort the meaning, but modifies the context. Here is the quote with the omissions inserted in brackets:

> [The question of good administration is related to the question of social structure, and] if you take some countries in Africa or Asia you find a curious structure. [You find an extremely poor farmer class, which is the great majority of the people; you find a small commercial class, for example; and] you find a small, leading group—intellectual, and very often with Western training [and so on.] But you have not got what we in the West call the fairly broad and solid middle class. [You have not got this in-between group] from which [I think, the universities and the colleges in the West and] the administrations in the West recruit most of their people. [You just have not got it.] That will come the [very] moment we get the proper kind of economic and social development. It will grow naturally, as it has grown in the West.[66]

Dismissing "Hammarskjöld's insistence elsewhere that each country had to 'find its own way, its own balance, its own form'", the critic claims that "this quotation reveals his ideas about the normal, desirable course of development: namely that new countries, if supported by the UN, would 'naturally' become more like 'the West'".[67] I must confess that my reading of this passage is different: reference is made to the absence of a social segment of the "middle class" in these societies, which through "the proper kind of economic and social development" would grow "naturally, as it has grown in the West". This does not seem to me to mean, as the critic claims, that such a class would be *like* that in the West, for example a *Western* middle class. It is also instructive to read the further answer which Hammarskjöld offered:

> But, waiting for that, we will be in a vicious circle, because you cannot get the proper substratum from which to recruit an administration without an economic improvement, and you cannot get economic improvement without having the people you can recruit from such a class. That is to say, we are in a kind of deadlock, and it seems to me that a good way out would be to offer our services.

Now I should add one thing, and that is, of course, that in this case as in other cases I would warn personally very strongly against the idea that we should go in any, let's say, paternal way and push this or that kind of proposal. An idea like this one, or a development like this one, is something which has to be asked for, properly understood, and sponsored primarily by the countries in need—not by the countries which wish to render services. That is to say, if I may go back to the phrase I used in reply to the representative of *The New York Times*, it is again a question of making an international service available. It is not a question of forcing an international service on these countries.[68]

Asked if he advocated "any particular system which might be better than another to bring all this about", he responded: "I think it has very little to do with ideologies or principles. Every country will find its own way, its own balance, its own form."[69]

In his speech he already had clarified:

Whatever may be our political philosophy we all recognize that it is impossible within any nation today to defend for long an inequality of economic conditions which the majority of the people believe to be unjust. This is true even when the average standard of living is so high that those who are less well off also have the possibility of a decent life. It is all the more true when conditions are such that the poorer people cannot meet the most elementary needs. Such differences render impossible the sound life of a nation ... One part of society should not live on gifts from the other part any more than one part of society should live on the exploitation of others.[70]

Perhaps not so "surprisingly", as the critic would believe, "there was no neat East/West or what one might today call global North/South divide in the discussions" regarding Hammarskjöld's proposal for an international administrative service introduced the same year.[71] That it took member states four more years to adopt his idea had presumably less to do with any suspicions of an ideological agenda, but more with the reluctance to delegate additional executive tasks to the Secretariat, which "put the UN in direct competition with the services offered by imperial powers designed to maintain ties with their former colonies".[72] While the practical impact was not great in view of the limited scale of support, critics point to its norm-setting effect: "UN initiatives and debates shaped what was soon recognized as the 'natural' course of decolonization, the needs of a newly independent or developing state, and the range of acceptable practices to meet these needs."[73] Hammarskjöld's thinking and approach certainly do not support such a conclusion. Rather, it borders on a preconceived perception that acknowledges the relative autonomy neither of the United Nations nor of its Secretary-General. In contrast, a recent thesis analysing the developmental role of the United Nations in terms of decolonisation and aid during the years 1949 to 1961

> avoids depicting the UN as a victim of classic Cold War machinations. Too many histories of this period take this approach by arguing that, to understand the actions of the UN, one needs to look no further than Washington, London, Moscow or Paris—and certainly not New York. This misrepresents the Organization's agency, particularly during the period under review ... The UN proved to be not just a handmaiden of developed member states, but a type of midwife for the birth of newly independent underdeveloped countries.[74]

If one considers the anti-colonial struggles and their nationalist discourses, the demands and goals articulated by the movements and their leaders, it is clear that the model of the nation state as rooted in the principle of the Westphalian order of sovereignty represented the kind of status aspired to in the struggles for independence. Taking Dag Hammarskjöld to task for his views as the second Secretary-General of the United Nations is tantamount to the proverbial tail wagging the dog. Instead, an alternative approach

> would situate Hammarskjöld's thought and practice within the post-war project of state formation and modernization that sought to universalize an idealized model of the liberal, welfare-oriented administrative state, particularly in formerly colonized territories. Though the precise form of such a state was contested, at its core was a governmental rationality and a common set of institutions that persist, in more or less attenuated form, to the present day. Hammarskjöld's significance lies precisely in his ability to articulate, within an evolving "constitutional" framework, a rationale of international authority that merged the moral justifications of that project of state formation and modernization with a novel assertion of the expertise of international civil servants in managing the attendant processes of decolonization and economic development.[75]

At the same time, such an approach "fostered a particular vision of the UN as an activist and interventionist organisation which should prevent the spread of the Cold War to the newly independent African and Asian nations, by providing them with a safe haven which would guarantee their sovereignty".[76]

6

THE SCOPE AND LIMITS OF DAG HAMMARSKJÖLD'S DIPLOMACY

The "great" commitment all too easily obscures the "little" one. But without the humility and warmth which you have to develop in your personal relations to the few with whom you are personally involved, you will never be able to do anything for the many.[1]

Two main case studies in this chapter illustrate the scope and limitations of Dag Hammarskjöld's diplomatic efforts to implement the United Nations Charter in the context of African decolonisation. More than any other engagement, the partial solution of the Suez crisis and the failure to end the conflict in the Congo during his time in office allow insights into the manoeuvring space available to him as well as the discrepancy between ambitions and realities. While the Suez crisis serves to illuminate what can be achieved by smart diplomacy, its success could not be repeated later on. To some extent it benefited from a moment of surprise, when Hammarskjöld managed to make use of an open window of opportunity.[2]

History does not always repeat itself. The greater emphasis in this chapter is therefore on the creation and execution of the mandate in the Congo. They demonstrate the role Hammarskjöld was able to play in a concrete situation with fundamentally conflicting interests presenting challenges and limits to his office—and where this role had its flaws.[3] As so often, such events and the actors involved invite very different stories and judgements: while some commentators praise Hammarskjöld for his diplomatic skills and relative success, others see him as a willing tool, remote-controlled by Western imperialist powers. Others again find a more nuanced assessment, which points to the limitations of such an office in a conflict in which all big powers had vested interests and hardly wanted the United Nations to set the agenda independently—even less so, to implement it without their say and control. By studying an account which presents the deliberations in New York, Hammarskjöld's reasoning and the situation on the ground, as well as giving voice to some others involved, readers may be able to draw their own conclusions. But before starting with Suez and the Congo, two other events towards the end of Hammarskjöld's time in office also illustrate the limits a UN Secretary-General faces in a situation where the powers involved refuse to collaborate in problem-solving.

Missions Unaccomplished: South Africa and Bizerte

The visit of Hammarskjöld to South Africa in January 1961 can on balance be considered as a failed attempt to address the apartheid regime's policy of racial discrimination. From what is known, it did not produce any meaningful direct results, and plans to follow up at a later stage were prevented by his untimely death.[4]

Racial discrimination in South Africa had already entered the agenda of the United Nations in its early years, albeit focused on the treatment of the Indian minority (see chapter three). Since the early 1950s the apartheid regime's oppression of the black majority emerged as a topical issue raised by the newly independent member states, alongside the continued occupation of South West Africa. But both matters remained at the margins and never managed to engage the Security Council.[5] On 10 December 1959, residents of the "Old Location" in Windhoek demonstrated against their planned forced removal to a new township further away from the city. Police killed 12 unarmed demonstrators and wounded over 50. Originally "the idea was floated that the UN Secretary-General might visit the territory, but nothing came of it, for the South African government was quick to hint that it would not welcome such a visit".[6]

Similarly, South Africa considered its apartheid policy of racial segregation a domestic affair, which would not justify any interference by the United Nations. The Sharpeville massacre of 21 March 1960,[7] when police opened fire on an unarmed crowd killing 69 people, marked a turning point and changed the dynamics of the situation. At the initiative of 29 African and

Asian member states, the Security Council condemned the South African government by nine votes with two abstentions (France and Great Britain).[8] It requested the Secretary-General to take the initiative in consultation with the government to uphold the purpose and principles of the Charter. Hammarskjöld interpreted this as a mandate to prepare for a visit and started to negotiate the terms for such a reconnaissance.[9] Exchanges with South Africa's foreign minister ended in arrangements stressing the "informal" nature of such a visit, limited only to consultations with the government. After several postponements Hammarskjöld finally visited South Africa from 6 to 12 January 1961, though the visit was overshadowed by the emerging crisis unfolding in the Congo. But his "movements were severely circumscribed and any contacts with people other than government representatives highly restricted".[10] Hammarskjöld

> held extensive discussions with Prime Minister Verwoerd, members of his cabinet, and leaders from the several racial communities. Despite these openings, however, Hammarskjöld admitted in his report to the Security Council that no mutual accepted arrangement for ending apartheid had been found "so far". The secretary-general did indicate that he expected to continue his discussions with the South African government and that he planned to return to South Africa for this purpose ... With his untimely passing, the unprecedented diplomatic opening Hammarskjold had created between his office and the Pretoria government on the apartheid issue lapsed for twenty-nine years.[11]

Another unresolved matter followed soon afterwards with the conflict over the French naval base at the Tunisian harbour town of Bizerte. Protests and demands for the French withdrawal from the occupied enclave escalated during July 1961 into a bloodbath, after paratroopers dispatched from France fired on the local population.[12] The event—and the lack of common ground—is documented in a few statements and cables that Hammarskjöld made as Secretary-General.[13] It is a classic example of how in the absence of sufficient support from all parties he was unable to take any meaningful action beyond a symbolic gesture by trying to visit the site of the conflict. But France simply ignored his efforts, prevented him from entering the naval base, and forced him to return without any result. This official attitude bordered on outright humiliation. Hammarskjöld's frustration is on record, not in official records of the United Nations, but in private correspondence. In what he called an "enormous letter" dated 31 July 1961,[14] he confided his utter disgust to Alexis Leger, a French diplomat and poet, with whom he had a close relationship sustained by private exchanges. For Hammarskjöld, the result of this defeat was that we are now witnesses to a tragedy that is not only Tunisia's, or [its president] Bourguiba's, but the tragedy of France and of the West. Because if France succeeds in keeping Bizerte for a few more years as a French base—and I don't really believe it can—France will have alienated that African opinion for which Bizerte now has the same importance as Suez, the feeling that France has really failed to maintain the moral principles that the West claims to defend. In the light of history as it presents itself in the eyes of the Arabs—which certainly would be told in a different way on the French side—it is very easy to understand the tragic sense of disappointment now felt by Bourgiba and those around him, who until now considered themselves as Europeans and as the French of Africa, and who maintain a high level of moral and political uprightness, despite the excess of emotion and the impatience they show.[15]

The letter also testifies to Hammarskjöld's strong personal dislike of Charles de Gaulle, which was beyond any doubt mutual.[16] De Gaulle, infuriated by the interventions by the United Nations in matters of French interest, considered the Secretary-General an "interloper", dismissing the United Nations as "the thing". The animosities dated back to the Suez crisis and were reinforced by the support the United Nations had offered Guinea through technical assistance and the presence of a special representative when refusing to accept the French terms of independence.[17]

The Suez Crisis

The Suez crisis can be considered a defining moment for the United Nations.[18] It offered Hammarskjöld the opportunity "to set up the UN as a neutral mediator and buffer between the Cold War opponents; as a broker in territorial and other conflicts between states; and as the fair defender of weak newcomers (such as Egypt) to the international system".[19] On 26 July 1956 Egypt's President Gamal Abdel Nasser announced the nationalisation of the Suez Canal. This brought an end to direct Western control over the strategic sea route. Hammarskjöld immediately engaged in exchanges with the foreign ministers of France, the UK and Egypt, as the most directly affected states, and on 13 October 1956 the Security Council officially endorsed an agreement regulating the future use of the canal. But the next day the French Prime Minister Guy Mollet, in a confidential exchange with his British counterpart, Anthony Eden, suggested a coordinated military action codenamed Operation Musketeer: Israel would attack Egypt from Sinai, thereby enabling France and Britain to regain control through direct negotiation and probable subsequent action, imposing their "solution" on

Egypt. On 29 October 1956 Israeli troops invaded and occupied Egyptian territory. This was in gross violation of the principles of the United Nations Charter and tantamount to a declaration of war. The move sabotaged Hammarskjöld's earlier diplomatic initiatives.

The military attack not only derailed the carefully designed and endorsed agreement, but also threatened to undermine the Secretary-General's authority. Hammarskjöld persuaded the US to call an urgent meeting of the Security Council. This took place on 30 and 31 October 1956. The first day saw several failed initiatives to reach a solution by breaking the impasse between the Israeli–French–British triumvirate and other Security Council members. Hammarskjöld sought to clear the blockage by introducing, through the Yugoslav delegate, a proposal to convene the General Assembly under the emergency procedure of the "Uniting for Peace'" resolution.[20] On 31 October 1956 he delivered a statement elaborating the principles that guided his under-standing of the execution of office. In personal notes[21] he observed: "the very least I could do was to play my position in order to get freedom of action in relation to the two permanent Members, which appeared to have put the UN aside, both in substance and in form".[22] Taking the floor, he presented his views in no uncertain terms, which have been quoted in chapter 4. He also stated: "As a servant of the Organization the Secretary-General has the duty to maintain his usefulness by avoiding public stands on conflicts between Member Nations unless and until such an action might help to resolve the conflict."[23] He clearly indicated his intention either to resign or at least to seek a vote of confidence, if Council members would not share his interpretation.[24]

In this way Hammarskjöld created a reference point that could not be ignored. All the delegations, including the permanent representatives of the UK, France and the Soviet Union, took the floor in the debate that followed and assured him, with varying levels of commitment, that he had their trust and support. With the support of the US and the Soviet Union, Hammarskjöld had in a sense outwitted France and the UK, who in the cir-cumstances were unable to block the "Uniting for Peace" procedure. At this moment a unique situation had been created, a window of opportunity that could not have been expected: "a man-bites-dog plot (the US and the Soviet Union join hands to defend Nasserist Egypt from an attack by Britain, France, and Israel—come again?)".[25] Hammarskjöld's bold initiative took advantage of a situation in which the foreign policies of the Soviet Union and the US alike were focused on globally more "open" economies rather than being con-fined to bilateral relations and controls. Because of this kind of "neo-colonial openness", "internationalists both in Moscow and Washington sought to undermine isolationist designs hatched in London and Paris".[26]

From 1 November 1956 the General Assembly held emergency sessions. These were the scene of much diplomatic wrangling within the Western bloc. Canada played a crucial role in the negotiations,[27] and was essential in bringing about the British and French willingness to stop military action. This was achieved on 2 November by persuading the UK and France to comply with the following arrangement, which was brought to the attention of the General Assembly the next day:

(a) Both the Egyptian and the Israel governments agree to accept a United Nations force to keep the peace;

(b) The United Nations decides to constitute and maintain such a force until an Arab–Israel peace settlement is reached and until satisfactory arrangements have been agreed in regard to the Suez Canal, both agreements to be guaranteed by the United Nations;

(c) In the meantime, until the United Nations force is constituted, both combatants agree to accept forthwith limited detachments of Anglo-French troops to be stationed between the combatants.[28]

Lester Pearson, then head of Canada's Permanent Mission, had other ideas from those the British and French assumed they had agreed to. Canada submitted a proposal for a United Nations force "large enough to keep [the] borders at peace while a political settlement [was] being worked out".[29] After some initial reluctance and following internal consultations with Pearson and his close staff members, Ralph Bunche and Andrew Cordier, Hammarskjöld warmed to the idea. On 3 November 1956 Canada, after being reassured that Egypt would agree to such a plan in principle, drafted a resolution in close coordination with Hammarskjöld. In this resolution the General Assembly

Requests, as a matter of priority, the Secretary-General to submit to it within forty-eight hours a plan for the setting up, with the consent of the nations concerned, of an emergency international United Nations force to secure and supervise the cessation of hostilities ...

Authorizes the Secretary-General immediately to arrange with the parties concerned for the implementation of the cease-fire and the halting of the movement of military forces and arms into the area and requests him to report compliance forthwith and, in any case, not later than twelve hours from the time of adoption of the present resolution ...[30]

The resolution was passed by 57 votes in favour, none against and 19 abstentions. This breakthrough was followed by an intense period of further negotiations over the details of the plan, in the course of which Hammarskjöld introduced the idea that the force would be under direct United Nations command and composed only of staff who were not permanent members of the Security Council. By 6 November 1956, Hammarskjöld had formulated five basic principles for peacekeeping missions. These were as follows:[31]

– Such a mission should be an emergency measure and limited in time.
– It would be carried out completely impartially and would not in any way be permitted to change or prejudice longer-term political or military power relationships, and force would be used only in self-defence.
– Permanent members of the Security Council would be excluded from the force.
– The mission would be under the command of a single United Nations officer.
– The deployment would require the consent of the parties involved, in particular the host country.

On 7 November 1956 the proposal gave birth to the United Nations Emergency Force (UNEF). It was the first peace mission under the direct control of the Secretary-General, having been approved by the General Assembly with 64 votes in favour, none against and 12 abstentions.

The UNEF operation achieved a degree of stability. Following negotiations between Hammarskjöld and Nasser on 16 and 17 November 1956, lasting for seven hours, Egypt finally accepted the character and mandate of the mission. "Good faith" was a decisive element of this success: Hammarskjöld conceded to Nasser the right to terminate the presence of UNEF in return for Nasser agreeing to endorse the mandate. Aware of the risk created by this concession, Hammarskjöld said in an internal note on 14 November 1956: "If we cannot base the United Nations action on a reasonable degree of good faith, then, of course, we have embarked on an extremely dangerous adventure."[32] The risk was confirmed by the Egyptian abrogation of the agreement in 1967 and the subsequent withdrawal of UNEF.

Although many people helped to create UNEF, Hammarskjöld has been widely praised for the decisive part played by his diplomatic skills and finesse: "UNEF's immediate success ... made the saying 'Leave it to Dag!' a slogan of international diplomacy."[33] The success came, however, at the price of strained relations with the British and the French. Hammarskjöld emerged more as a General than a Secretary in serving the United Nations Charter. While this strengthened his position, it prompted some of the most influential member states to see him as a risk when their interests were at stake. Describing him as "the artist of the peaceful resolution of the Suez crisis", Manuel Fröhlich argues that his means "were not tangible resources of power, but rather moral force that subsequently came to be the classical rationale of numerous peacekeeping missions".[34] But moral force may not be enough in a complex situation where the parties have such strong interests that they are unlikely to be impressed and influenced by soft power. After all, their interests and their realpolitik are hardly ever guided by morality—at best by a pseudo-morality used as pretext for agenda-setting. The Congo was such a situation. This case study shows that even as skilled a diplomat as Hammarskjöld could not find a lasting solution. While his views and arguments might have come in handy for some, they did not endorse them because of an absence of self-interest.

The Congo Operations

What had first been "King Leopold's empire" and then the Belgian Congo obtained formal independence on 30 June 1960. President Joseph Kasavubu and Prime Minister Patrice Lumumba led the Congolese government when independence was declared. Only days into national sovereignty, Congolese soldiers embarked on a series of mutinies against the Belgian officers still in control of the military.[35] While Kasavubu and Lumumba negotiated a reshuffle of the army command, the Belgian government dispatched paratroopers to the Katanga province and other places on 10 July. Katanga's mineral wealth was of major geostrategic importance and was mainly exploited by the Belgian mining company Union Minière du Haut Katanga and other Western mining companies. The Belgian military intervention, requested by the Katangese provincial president, Moise Tshombe, was in violation of an agreement between Belgium and the Congo entered into at independence. On 11 July, Tshombe proclaimed the independence of Katanga from the Congo. This secession and subsequent military clashes with Belgian paratroopers caused Kasavubu and Lumumba in a telegram of 12 July to request of the Secretary-General the "urgent dispatch by the United Nations of military assistance". Blaming Belgium for masterminding the secession of Katanga, the essential purpose of the request was "to protect the national territory of the Congo against the present external aggression".[36] A follow-up cable to the Secretary-General on 13 July clarified that

(1) the purpose of the aid requested is not to restore the internal situation in Congo but rather to protect the national territory against acts of aggression committed by Belgian metropolitan troops.

(2) The request for assistance relates only to a United Nations force consisting of military personnel from neutral countries ...

(3) If the assistance requested is not received without delay the Republic of the Congo will be obliged to appeal to the Bandung treaty powers.[37]

This was intended to avoid the risk that United Nations forces might collaborate with the Belgian military on the ground. It set in motion a hitherto unprecedented involvement of the United Nations in matters of a member state.[38]

The Mandate and Its Implementation

Hammarskjöld acted immediately. For the first time invoking Article 99 of the Charter,[39] he brought the issue before the Security Council by calling for an urgent meeting the same evening, and "thereby inscribed it on the global security agenda".[40] As he argued: "The difficulties which have developed in the Congo ... have an important international bearing as they are of a nature that cannot be disregarded by other countries." For him, "the presence of the Belgian troops cannot be accepted as a satisfactory stopgap arrangement pending the reestablishment of order through the national security force". He suggested that "the United Nations Force would not be authorized to action beyond self-defence" and "that they may not take any action which would make them a party to internal conflicts". He expressed his intention "to get, in the first place, assistance from African nations" and finally urged the Council "to act with the utmost speed".[41]

After intense negotiations, the following draft resolution was tabled by Tunisia:

The Security Council,

Considering the report of the Secretary-General on a request for United Nations action in relation to the Republic of the Congo,

Considering the request for military assistance addressed to the Secretary-General by the President and the Prime Minister of the Republic of the Congo (S/4382),

1. *Calls upon* the Government of Belgium to withdraw its troops from the territory of the Republic of the Congo;

2. *Decides* to authorize the Secretary-General to take the necessary steps, in consultation with the Government of the Republic of the Congo, to provide the government with such military assistance as may be necessary until, through the efforts of the Congolese government with the technical assis-

tance of the United Nations, the national security forces may be able, in the opinion of the government, to meet fully their task;

3. *Requests* the Secretary-General to report to the Security Council as appropriate.[42]

The text was controversially discussed but finally adopted by eight votes (US, USSR, Argentina, Ceylon, Ecuador, Italy, Poland and Tunisia) with the abstention of France, Britain and Nationalist China. But the US and the Soviet permanent representatives indicated the existence of conflicting interpretations in their explanatory statements: "Lodge [of the US] said the resolution made Belgian withdrawal contingent upon creation and deployment of the UN Force. Sobolev [of the USSR] said the resolution should be interpreted as calling for immediate and unconditional Belgian withdrawal."[43]

The resolution was the result of a necessary compromise, which avoided the looming veto of any of the permanent members (this risk was also reduced by having Tunisia submit the text). But as the interpretations showed, misunderstandings existed from the beginning as regards the limitations of the mandate:

> The miracle of the success of the Security Council could not hide the weaknesses of the text that was agreed upon, despite the Cold War constraints of the time, precisely because it left room for at least two different interpretations. According to Western countries and, to a certain extent, to the Secretary-General, the UN operation should assist the Congolese government to maintain internal order, whereas the Soviet Union, Poland and Tunisia thought of it as an instrument to help the Congolese government to face Belgian aggression.[44]

The complicated situation, which required a formulation that would create (despite differing interpretations) the impression of some kind of common purpose, brought about the authorisation of a military presence in the country without any clear and concrete guidelines. While the resolution provided space for manoeuvring—at times deliberately used by Hammarskjöld at his discretion—it also created the risk that, in the absence of clarity, at different moments all of the parties involved would become critical of what the Secretariat did: "in directing the Secretary-General to eliminate any justification for foreign intervention by restoring law and order, as far as possible with the help of the Congo government but without using force or interfering in internal affairs, the Council from the start injected an inherent contradiction into the Congo operation".[45]

The Secretariat acted immediately and established Opération des Nations Unies au Congo (ONUC) as a multinational peacekeeping force. Its conceptualisation and implementation were—considering the communication technologies of those days—surprisingly efficiently handled. US transport planes arrived on 15 July—30 hours after the Security Council resolution had been adopted—with a first contingent of Tunisian soldiers, followed by troops from Ghana, Ethiopia and Morocco. When Hammarskjöld presented his first report to the Security Council on 18 July, 3,500 ONUC troops had arrived in Léopoldville. Already then, the initial differing interpretations necessitated a clarifying statement by the Secretary-General. As he explained, "on the basis of the interpretation I had given, it would be understood that, were the United Nations to act as I proposed, the Belgian government 'would see its way to a withdrawal', and the Council itself called upon the Belgian government to withdraw its troops". At the same time, he stressed that the ONUC force was "not under the orders of the [Congolese] government nor can it ... be permitted to become a party to any internal conflict".[46] While this was met with reservations by African countries, who suspected backtracking on the issue of Katanga, Hammarskjöld only two days later tried to reassure the Security Council of the intention to restore the territorial integrity of the Congo: "The resolution of the Security Council in response to the appeal from the Government of the Congo clearly applies to the whole of the Territory of the Republic as it existed when the Security Council, only a few days earlier, recommended the Congo for admission as a Member of the United Nations."[47]

He also suggested that the Security Council reinforce and clarify the mandate as regards the withdrawal of Belgian troops. He observed that "the Security Council did not, as it has done in previous cases, authorize or request the Secretary-General to take specific steps for the implementation of withdrawal—apart, of course, from the establishment of the Force", but understood his mandate as the "implementation of its decision on withdrawal". And he continued: "Although I do not consider it necessary, a clarification of my mandate ... would be useful by the Council. Such a clarification, if made, might aim at establishing the substance of my mandate on this point and the aim of the Council as regards the implementation of the call for a withdrawal."[48]

Another draft resolution, again submitted by Tunisia's permanent representative, Mongi Slim, as Africa's spokesperson in the Security Council, was subsequently adopted on 22 July as Resolution 145(1960). It

1. *Calls upon* the Government of Belgium to implement speedily the Security Council resolution of July 14, 1960 on the withdrawal of its troops, and authorizes the Secretary-General to take all necessary action to this effect.

2. *Requests* all States to refrain from any action which might tend to impede the restoration of law and order and the exercise by the Government of the Congo of its authority and also to refrain from any action which might undermine the territorial integrity and the political independence of the Republic of the Congo.[49]

By the end of July 1960, the ONUC contingent on the ground amounted to 11,155 soldiers from Ethiopia, Ghana, Guinea, Ireland, Liberia, Morocco, Sweden and Tunisia. Another battalion from Mali was due to arrive and about 60 pilots for the United Nations airlift were provided by Argentina, Brazil, Ethiopia, India, Norway, Sweden and Yugoslavia.[50] While the first steps suggested a rather smooth translation of the mandate into action, Hammarskjöld was confronted with major obstacles. In early August efforts to station troops in Katanga failed. Tshombe declared that any entry of ONUC troops would be met with military resistance, while the Belgian government declared its "submission" to the Security Council resolutions. Hammarskjöld interpreted this "to mean only absence of active resistance", which "presents us with a serious problem, especially in a situation like the one now created by Mr. Tshombe".[51] He also pointed to another dilemma:

> The central government, in its turn, has shown great impatience. When I presented to them the reasons why, while acting with the utmost speed, I could not responsibly act more speedily, from many quarters the reaction has been one of distrust ... thus creating a harmful atmosphere against the major effort of the United Nations in active support of the Republic of the Congo. This dangerous tendency of sowing distrust has not been without support from other quarters outside the Congo.[52]

After lengthy debates, a third resolution adopted on 9 August 1960 confirmed the authority vested in the Secretary-General and "requests him to carry out the responsibility placed on him". It urged the government of Belgium to withdraw its troops from Katanga immediately, declared (3) that the entry of the United Nations force into Katanga was necessary to implement the resolution fully, and reaffirmed that the ONUC force "will not be a party to or in any way intervene in or be used to influence the outcome of any internal conflict, constitutional or otherwise", while at the same time it referred to Articles 25[53] and 49[54] of the UN Charter to call upon member states "to accept and carry out the decisions".[55]

But the situation on the ground became increasingly complicated. After his arrival in Léopoldville to initiate the necessary measures, including a visit to Elisabethville to meet Moise Tshombe, Hammarskjöld was confronted with expectations which in his view required clarification of the mission's impartiality. He released an interpretation of paragraph 4 of the Security Council's third resolution and concluded "that the United Nations Force cannot be used on behalf of the central government to subdue or to force the provincial government to a specific line of action".[56] As a result, the cordial relations with Lumumba ended abruptly, since he felt betrayed, and he accused Hammarskjöld of taking sides with the Belgians and Tshombe. He declared a state of emergency and appealed for help from the Soviet Union to prepare for an invasion of Katanga. On two occasions, soldiers of the Congolese national army attacked ONUC staff. The rift between Hammarskjöld and the Congolese government as represented by the Lumumba faction manifested itself when the Security Council debated the matter on 21 August. In response to Hammarskjöld's opening statement, the Congolese government's representative, Antoine Gizenga, complained that, "if the resolutions of the Security Council continue to be badly interpreted, this will not lead to the liberation of the Congo but to the effective reconquest of the country".[57] Hammarskjöld in reply clarified some issues he considered as "misinformation" and rebutted the accusation that he had not sufficiently consulted the Congolese government by reminding Gizenga "that the relations between the Secretary-General and the Council are not to be interfered with by any government". And he added, "I went to the Security Council in the best interest of the central government of the Congo".[58] Finally, after two more critical interventions by Guinea and the USSR, both asking for more military support for Lumumba and the delegation of some military responsibilities in the ONUC operations to the Congolese army, Hammarskjöld elaborated further:

> There is one point which has also been raised in some interventions, and that is the question of national governments' wishes as regards the employment of their troops. I think it must be clear that military operations of this kind have to be under a unified command exercising its authority and its judgement as best it can. If we were to try to meet desires expressed by the very many participating governments, then I think that operation would very soon come to a deadlock.[59]

With the exception of the Soviet Union and Poland, all Council members (including Tunisia and Ceylon as spokespersons for Africa and Asia), after the three statements of Hammarskjöld clarifying his view, finally supported his conduct of the operation. But this did not solve the impasse.

The rift that erupted between President Kasavubu and Lumumba resulted in the latter's dismissal as Prime Minister on 5 September 1960. This caused a deep division in the national government. The ensuing fights over the control

of government ended with the assassination of Lumumba and two of his closest allies. At the same time, the continued Belgian presence and that of foreign
mercenaries in Katanga encouraged Tshombe to remain stubbornly non-
compliant with the demand to reintegrate the province into the territory of
the Congo. Faced with these obstacles, Hammarskjöld and the ONUC force
came under growing pressure from the divergent interests of the member
states to deliver what was expected. This bordered at times on the dictum
"damned if you do, damned if you don't".

Lumumba's dismissal was triggered by his turn towards the USSR as an ally.
This created fears among other members of government, making them willing
to succumb to US influence to get rid of the popular leader. In the absence of
US support, which he had tried in vain to secure during a visit in July,
Lumumba accepted massive military aid willingly offered by the Soviet
Union: "The Soviet deliveries included hundred [sic] of trucks with spare
parts, while the number of Soviet planes supplied to Lumumba is still
unclear."[60] The equipment was immediately used for deployment in mid-
August 1960 to enable the Congolese army to crush the secession of Kasai.
The "Mining State of South Kasai", bordering on Katanga in the north, had
declared its autonomy on 8 August with the support of the Belgians and the
mining companies. From there the government troops were supposed to move
on to Katanga. "But the National Army was dragged into ethnic fighting in
Kasai between the Baluba and the Bena Lulua. What was originally an offensive to end the secession of Kasai and Katanga saw a series of massacres in
which the Congolese National Army was involved."[61]

Reporting to the Security Council, Hammarskjöld reacted within days in
a statement which was originally prepared independently and motivated by
the need to secure voluntary contributions to a United Nations fund for
financial assistance to the Republic of the Congo:

11. The internal conflicts, which have become increasingly grave in the last few
weeks and even days, have taken on a particularly serious aspect due to the
fact that parties have relied on and obtained certain assistance from the
outside, contrary to the spirit of the Security Council resolutions and tend-
ing to reintroduce elements of the very kind the Security Council wished to
eliminate when it requested the immediate withdrawal of Belgian troops.
The conflicts have further led to considerable losses of human lives and to
continued danger for human lives in forms which sometimes have been of
great brutality, contrary to the principles established and maintained by the
United Nations.

12. In view of this dual aggravating aspect of the internal conflicts, I consider it
essential, as part of the widened and intensified effort for which I appeal in

this report, that the Security Council reaffirm its request to all states to refrain from any action which might tend to impede the restoration of law and order or to aggravate differences, and that it clarify, in appropriate terms, the mandate of the United Nations.[62]

The Council only met to discuss the report on 9 September. By then, the dismissal of Lumumba and the role of ONUC had become highly controversial. The same day the Soviet government "strongly criticized the command of the ONUC and Hammarskjold in particular. The UN General Secretary, the statement reads, 'has turned out to be the part of the organization's machinery which openly works to the advantage of colonizers, thus comprising the UN.'"[63]

In his opening statement to the Council session, Hammarskjöld supported the decisions taken by his special representative Andrew Cordier, who closed down Leopoldville radio station, thus preventing anyone from broadcasting messages, and closed the airports for all but United Nations operations:

> The two far-reaching steps of an emergency nature which were taken by the United Nations representatives were, as I have already said, not preceded by a consultation with the authorities. Nor could they have been. But further, they were not preceded by any reference to the matter to me, because of the extreme urgency of the problem our people were facing on the spot. This latter fact throws, in my view, considerable light on the character of a situation which it is easy to sit in New York and discuss in terms of protocol, but which it requires wisdom and courage to handle when you are at the front. Anyway, it should be clear that the steps taken cannot be discussed in terms of partisanship, colonialism, or anticolonialism.[64]

After more toing and froing in the Security Council, a draft resolution introduced by Ceylon and Tunisia and supported by the African and Asian member states on 16 September was vetoed by the Soviet Union and Poland. At the proposal of the US delegate an emergency special session of the General Assembly was convened the next day. The Soviet permanent representative continued his personal attacks on Hammarskjöld, which he had already started during the Security Council sessions, using even sharper language. Hammarskjöld responded twice during the three-day debate, which even provoked collisions between the Afro-Asian and the Soviet blocs. In the end, an Afro-Asian resolution was accepted, which requested "all states to refrain from any action which might tend to impede the restoration of law and order and the exercise by the Government of the Republic of the Congo of its authority and also to refrain from any action which might undermine the unity, territorial integrity and the political independence of the Republic of the Congo".[65] Hammarskjöld commented:

I have been happy indeed to note the correspondence between the attitude reflected in the resolution and that of the Secretariat as presented most recently in the fourth report. I believe that I am right in finding in this fact evidence of a fundamental and encouraging agreement with and within the African world regarding the aims and the very philosophy of this major United Nations operation.[66]

Far from a de-escalation, this was only the prelude to what followed with the opening of the fifteenth annual session of the General Assembly on 20 September. Speaking on 23 September, Soviet leader Nikita Khrushchev attacked "the colonialists", who "have been doing their dirty work in the Congo through the Secretary-General of the United Nations and his staff". He asked the Assembly to "call Mr. Hammarskjöld to order and ensure that he does not misuse the position of the Secretary-General but carries out his functions in strict accordance with the provisions of the United Nations Charter and the decisions of the Security Council".[67] He then introduced a proposal to replace the Secretary-General with a tripartite executive. Such a troika would be composed of one representative from each of the Western, the Socialist and the non-aligned blocs. This went beyond the Congo affair by targeting the structure of the Secretariat. When the general debate resumed, Hammarskjöld was the first speaker: "The question before the General Assembly", he stated, "is no longer one of certain actions but one of the principles guiding them".

> This is a question not of a man but of an institution. Use whatever words you like, independence, impartiality, objectivity—they all describe essential aspects of what, without exception, must be the attitude of the Secretary-General. Such an attitude, which has found its clear and decisive expression in Article 100 of the Charter, may at any stage become an obstacle for those who work for certain political aims which would be better served or more easily achieved if the Secretary-General compromised with this attitude. But if he did, how gravely he would then betray the trust of all those for whom the strict maintenance of such attitude is their best protection in the world-wide fight for power and influence. ...

> Sometimes one gets the impression that the Congo operation is looked at as being in the hands of the Secretary-General, as somehow distinct from the United Nations. No: this is your operation, gentlemen. And this is true whether you represent the African and Asian Member countries, which carry the main burden for the Force and for its command, or speak and act for other parts of the world. There is nothing in the Charter, which puts responsibility of this kind on the shoulders of the Secretary-General or makes him the independent master of such an operation ... It is for you to indicate what you want to have done. As

the agent of the Organization I am grateful for any positive advice, but if no such positive advice is forthcoming ... then I have no choice but to follow my own conviction, guided by the principles to which I have just referred.[68]

In speeches on 1 and 3 October, Khrushchev continued to attack Hammarskjöld, and finally called upon him to resign. Hammarskjöld's response would become the most famous of his speeches and contributed to his iconic status. Twice during his announcement, he was interrupted by long applause and a standing ovation, in which the key representatives of the non-aligned countries prominently demonstrated their support.

It is not the Soviet Union or indeed any other Big Powers which need the United Nations for their protection. It is all the others. In this sense, the Organization is first of all their Organization and I deeply believe in the wisdom with which they will be able to use it and guide it. I shall remain in my post during the term of office as a servant of the Organization in the interest of all those other nations as long as they wish me to do so.[69]

Khrushchev had made a strategic mistake by trying to use the ousting of Lumumba to suggest the replacement of Hammarskjöld by a troika: "The Afro-Asian states did not support this plan since they considered it to be nothing more than diplomatic manoeuvring and propaganda. The USSR failed to create a pro-Lumumba international coalition as a counterweight to the UN forces."[70] But while Hammarskjöld's resilience was rewarded by the demonstrative solidarity of the leaders of the African and Asian member states, there was also a flip-side: "Hammarskjöld, by opposing Khrushchev publicly finally, became a heroic figure in the West—which was the last thing he wanted to be."[71]

The Assassination of Patrice Lumumba

The dilemma created by the notion of neutrality became obvious when Lumumba was ousted from office as Prime Minister and the Congolese government soon thereafter fell apart. Hammarskjöld and the Secretariat were confronted with the need to respond. The Congo mission was in terms of its mandate supposed to act in consultation with the constitutional government. But when President Kasavubu and Prime Minister Lumumba clashed in early September 1960, the question was who, by virtue of his position, could claim to legitimately represent the government. Hammarskjöld followed the legal advice he had asked for in the Secretariat and concluded that the provisional constitution for the Congo, the Loi Fondamentale, allowed the Chief of

State (the President), under Article 22, to dismiss the Prime Minister and appoint a new one if his action was endorsed by at least one minister. This had been the case in the dismissal of Lumumba: as one of the highest-ranking officials serving at the time in the Secretariat said: "For all practical purposes, it seemed that in the present circumstances the UN must inevitably regard the Chief of State as the only unquestioned constitutional authority."[72] Resisting at the same time demands to end the secession of Katanga by force and to reinstate Lumumba, Hammarskjöld "declared that ONUC was not for rent".[73] "Already Hammarskjöld was labouring hard ... on scholastic hair-splitting arguments about what type of sovereignty should be respected and what type should not. His clutching at straws was that the UN had no interests of its own in intervention; the UN was intervening on the authority of a Security Council resolution."[74]

But this did not mean that Hammarskjöld would not give recognition to Lumumba, whom he considered influential and a relevant counterpart. When, as a result of intense lobbying by the UK and the US, the General Assembly awarded the status of member state to the Kasavubu government on 22 November 1960, Hammarskjöld was "appalled" by the spectacle.[75] Handing sole legitimacy to Kasavubu may well have been the original, if not decisive, step towards the later physical elimination of Lumumba. Part of the reason for the intense campaign for the recognition of Kasavubu, including arm-twisting of dependent states by the Anglo-American axis, "was the recognition that Hammarskjöld regarded Lumumba as the legitimate Prime Minister. Discussions with the Secretary-General had revealed that despite the animosity of relations with Lumumba, by the middle of October, no doubt due to the pressure from the Afro-Asian states, Hammarskjöld had come to the position that no solution to the Congo was possible without him."[76]

Lumumba decided at the end of November to leave his residence, in which he was temporarily under the protection of the Blue Helmets, to mobilise for his return into power. While the Kasavubu government and the new army strongman, Mobutu Sésé Seko, who had been involved in the ousting of Lumumba, stood by, Lumumba—with the involvement of the CIA, Belgian soldiers and mercenaries—was captured in early December and flown to Léopoldville. Witnessing his detention, a contingent of soldiers from Ghana remained passive in the absence of any authorised intervention. Detained for weeks in the Thysville military barracks several hundred miles away from the capital, Lumumba was flown to Elisabethville on 17 January 1961 together with fellow prisoners Maurice Mpolo and Joseph Okito. A Swedish United

Nations detail of six men observed the group's arrival across the airfield, but their identity was only confirmed the next day. The three were tortured and finally executed by a firing squad the same night.[77] The crime was covered up for some time and news confirming Lumumba's death reached New York only on 13 February 1961.

For Nikita Khrushchev, the non-interference of the ONUC forces on the ground was another confirmation that Hammarskjöld was a lackey of Western interests. As we have seen, Hammarskjöld had been blamed personally for not restoring Lumumba's role in the government of the Congo and was later also held responsible for his killing. But Hammarskjöld had not sat by. He wrote on 3 December 1960 to President Kasavubu expressing concern that action against Lumumba "would be taken contrary to recognized rules of law" and that this "would seriously put in jeopardy the international prestige of the Republic of the Congo and mean a most serious blow to principles to be upheld by the United Nations and their Members".[78] In a second letter on 5 December he referred to the Charter principle concerning "respect for human rights and for fundamental freedoms for all". He then added a reference to Article 66 of the Congolese Fundamental Law on parliamentary immunity, since Lumumba and others detained "are members of one or the other Chamber of Parliament". Referring to eyewitnesses observing "physical violence and degrading treatment" particularly against Lumumba, he urged that the "International Red Cross be asked to examine the detained persons and their places and conditions of detention and otherwise to obtain the necessary assurances for their safety".[79] In a letter dated 7 December, Kasavubu rejected the proposal. The same day, Hammarskjöld opened the Security Council's session and responded at length to the criticism of partiality, stating:

> The United Nations sent troops and civilian technicians to the Congo for clearly defined Charter aims and under clearly defined Charter principles ... The Organization, in pursuit of this aim, should maintain a position of strict neutrality in relation to all domestic problems of a political nature into which the Organization under the Charter had no right to interfere ...
>
> That does not mean, of course, that I claim any infallibility for what the United Nations has done in the Congo—naturally, mistakes have been made—but what I do claim is that such possible mistakes have not reflected any change of policy implying a departure from the aims and principles proper to the Organization.[80]

In several more sessions during December, the Security Council was unable to adopt any of the draft resolutions presented and amended, while Hammarskjöld on several occasions sought to explain over and over again the need for a clear mandate, stressing the view that the Secretariat was bound only to such a mandate and the underlying principles of the Charter.

When on 18 January the news reached to New York that Lumumba and two other prisoners had been seen arriving in Katanga, Hammarskjöld sent messages on 19 January to President Kasavubu and Moise Tshombe urging that the prisoners be transferred to Léopoldville in the interest of a fair trial. In a second letter to Kasavubu on 20 January he maintained:

> negotiations cannot be conducted among political leaders as long as some of them are detained, and thus unable in freedom to express their views or to take part in deliberations. This general observation, which is amply justified by experience, has special application in the present situation where, as is well known, one of those incarcerated commands a high position in wide sections of the public which would make any solution arrived at without proper contact with him unstable.[81]

At that time, as we know today, the corpses of the three victims had already been dismembered beyond recognition.

To what extent the passivity of the United Nations worked at least indirectly to support Western interests in removing Lumumba from office and finally eliminating him physically—by means of an intervention through non-intervention—remains a contested matter. It also remains a matter of controversy to what extent the United Nations should have protected Lumumba even after he had decided to leave at his own risk the residence in which he stayed under ONUC protection. As Hammarskjöld and others argued, by leaving a secure house to mobilise for the restoration of his political influence, Lumumba became involved again in Congolese politics as the result of his own decision. Protecting him in this role could have been interpreted as tantamount to undue interference in the political affairs of the country and therefore a violation of the mandated neutrality. As has been argued in retrospect:

> Hammarskjöld's difficulties in providing security to Lumumba stemmed from a number of developments. These included (1) the inability of the U.N. to counter activities of some foreign embassies in the Congo, which were actively opposed to Lumumba, (2) ONUC efforts to avoid a major military confrontation between its troops and the Congolese army, which would have been necessary to bring Lumumba out of Congolese custody, and (3) the possibility of Lumumba being killed during a rescue operation.[82]

Critics like De Witte claim that if it were not for the passive role of the United Nations, "the assassination could never have been carried out".[83] A response to this accusation by Brian Urquhart, a former member of the staff close to Hammarskjöld,[84] provoked the reiteration that "Secretary-General Hammarskjöld played a decisive role in the overthrow of the Congolese government of Patrice Lumumba", thereby willingly accepting Lumumba's assassination.[85] In his response, Urquhart described De Witte's "elaborate fantasy of Hammarskjöld's conspiracy with the Belgians" as "absurd to anyone who worked with Hammarskjöld at the time and experienced his frustration and his frequent rages at, and denunciations of, both the Belgians and their protégé, the Katangese leader, Moïse Tshombe".[86] Colin Legum, a credible witness, joined this controversy. He claimed to have spoken to a stressed and intoxicated Lumumba, who acted rather irrationally hours before abandoning United Nations protection. In Legum's view this "discounts the many erroneous versions of what happened given by critics who have sought to show UN collaboration in Lumumba's ghastly fate".[87]

But there were indeed disturbing contradictions and inconsistencies, which suggest that the intervention in the Congo was at times very dependent upon individuals rather than being an organised and concerted action based on a clear strategy. The situation was at times confusing, while often requiring quick action, which risked being wrong. Communication with varying competing Congolese factions was at best complicated. Exasperation was at times a crucial factor, making even the highest-ranking officials in their interactions with local counterparts "more impatient and less diplomatic than they might have been in a more normal situation".[88] Initiatives on an ad hoc basis by locally deployed civilian and military staff were not always endorsed by Hammarskjöld, who "didn't know what his people were doing, had no idea of what they were getting into, and would certainly have violently disapproved of it if he had known".[89]

The "Congo Club", those higher staff members who were directly involved in the operations both in the Secretariat and on the ground, most notably the Americans Ralph Bunche and Andrew Cordier, the Irishman Conor Cruise O'Brien and the Indian Rajeshwar Dayal, as well as the Swedish commander of the Blue Helmet forces, Carl von Horn (who due to a dismal performance was replaced at the end of 1960), created a special mix, in which at times personal chemistry played an important though rather negative if not destructive role. The personal account of Conor Cruise O'Brien[90] provides a detailed narrative illustrating "how an international civil service can be forged from men whose national cultures and working experience necessarily have a heavy hold on their minds".[91] Critical assessments of the Congo mission of the early 1960s observe that the officials with the most influential decision-making impact "shared a common Cold War outlook with Western policy makers, and saw their mission in the Congo as that of preserving the then existing balance of forces in the world".[92] Ralph Bunche's interaction with Patrice Lumumba was a particularly negative example of clashes in personal chemistry, with suspicions on both sides and miscommunication. Diagnosed as a "fatal encounter", the mismatch between Bunche and Lumumba had a tragic outcome: much as "the flow of information that shaped their understandings was so completely at odds that one might imagine that they were engaged in wholly separate settings".[93] As ridiculous as it sounds, the exchanges between the Afro-American Bunche and the Congolese Pan-African nationalist Lumumba displayed strong racist undertones on both sides. Bunche "remained a fervent lifelong opponent of black nationalism, whether in the United States or abroad, and much of his antagonism to the anticolonial nationalist Patrice Lumumba in the Congo stemmed from his visceral dislike of all forms of celebration of *négritude*".[94]

Such a situation may "wittingly or unwittingly" have "provided to those seeking Lumumba's demise the justification and the opportunities they needed to remove a democratically elected leader from office by illegal means"[95]— with deadly consequences. There seems to be, however, no convincing evidence that this happened with the authorisation or even acceptance of Dag Hammarskjöld. Arguments along this line lack credible sources. An article by Carole Collins suggests that "the U.N. leadership—personified by Cordier and Hammarskjöld—was so preoccupied with global East–West concerns that it remained blind to the implications of its actions for the decolonization and democratization of Africa", being guided only by "the logic of global politics within an anti-communist framework that Cordier and Hammarskjöld accepted without question".[96] But this article offers not a single reference to Hammarskjöld's position. It is based exclusively on a few letters by Cordier to a close friend and college mentor written in 1960–1, now deposited in the A.W. Cordier Collection at Columbia University. These allow first-hand insights into Cordier's anti-communist stance and his role in the Congo at the crucial moment when Lumumba was ousted from his office as Prime Minister. But not once does any reference to Hammarskjöld feature in the quotes from the letters, despite the author constantly referring to "Hammarskjöld and Cordier" as if they had been and acted like Siamese twins. On the contrary, they rather seem to confirm what Hammarskjöld had stated in the Security Council on 9 September 1960, that the decisions by Cordier were taken without any preceding consultation and in the absence of any instructions from

New York. Nevertheless, this does not exonerate the United Nations from any blame. Rather, Lumumba's horrible end testified to the fact that the consequences of the UN's activities (or passivity) were at times determined by the individuals on the ground acting on the organisation's behalf. Perhaps a fair assessment has been offered in retrospect by Brian Urquhart:

> The assassination of Lumumba was a brutal and squalid atrocity. It was engineered by Mobutu and by the Belgian government in an effort to re-establish their influence and to protect its interests in the Congo. The assassination was condoned by the United States, which feared that Lumumba was becoming an African Fidel Castro. The UN, with its policy of non-interference in the internal politics of the Congo, failed to rescue Lumumba at the one point—his arrest at Mweka—when it might possibly have been able to do so. Nobody comes out well in this story.[97]

In a letter to John Steinbeck, Hammarskjöld commented on the news of Lumumba's assassination as follows: "I incline to the conclusion that *no* one, in the long pull, will really profit from Lumumba's death, least of all those outside the Congo who now strain to do so but should one day confront a reckoning with truth and decency."[98] As Brian Urquhart remembered: "Hammarskjöld was completely stuck with this, and it was a terrible situation. I think it took a great toll on him; he became extremely irascible, extremely emotional, on this subject—I think with good reason—and it really was a very gloomy time. It was pretty awful."[99]

Contested Neutrality and Military Operations

Increasingly under attack by the Soviet Union and its allies, but also facing mixed reactions from the non-aligned states, Hammarskjöld denied allegations that the United Nations was acting in compliance with Western interests, but insisted on the need for neutrality and non-intervention in domestic politics. This did not ease the constant pressure on the ONUC operations exerted by the many different parties involved. These included the variety of Western interests as represented most prominently by Belgium but also by the United Kingdom and France (already at crossed swords with the Hammarskjöld diplomacy since the Suez intervention) and the US, the British settler colonial minority regimes of the Central African Federation (Northern and Southern Rhodesia and Nyasaland) and apartheid South Africa, as well as the opposing interests of the Soviet camp in securing a stake in the resource-rich territory—or at least preventing the West from establishing another satellite regime. Matters became even more complicated as a result of a policy change on the part of the US administration under President J.F. Kennedy, who came to office in early 1961. He deviated from earlier US foreign policy under Dwight D. Eisenhower by seeking closer relations with the newly independent African countries and was "eager [to] produce a Congo situation more acceptable to African and international opinion".[100]

Following the news of the murder of Patrice Lumumba, Maurice Mpolo and Joseph Okito, Hammarskjöld discussed the situation in a series of meetings from 13 February 1961. On 15 February he did not mince his words when he voiced his frustration over the accusations levelled against the United Nations mission and the renewed Soviet demands for his resignation:

> For seven or eight months, through efforts far beyond the imagination of those who founded this Organization, [the UN's Secretariat and the Office of the Secretary-General] has tried to counter tendencies to introduce the Big-Power conflict into Africa and put the young African countries under the shadow of the cold war. It has done so with great risks and against heavy odds. It has done so at the cost of very great personal sacrifices for a great number of people. In the beginning the effort was successful, and I do not now hesitate to say that on more than one occasion the drift into a war with foreign-power intervention of the Korean or Spanish type was avoided only thanks to the work done by the Organization, basing itself on African solidarity. We effectively countered efforts from all sides to make the Congo a happy hunting ground for national interests. To be a roadblock to such efforts is to make yourself the target of attacks from all those who find their plans thwarted ... From both sides the main accusation was a lack of objectivity. The historian will undoubtedly find in this balance of accusations the very evidence of that objectivity we were accused of lacking, but also of the fact that very many Member nations have not yet accepted the limits put on their national ambitions by the very existence of the United Nations and by the membership of that Organization.[101]

The turn towards a "politics of murder"[102] was a watershed, "as it brought about a sharp revision in the concept of the methods to be employed by the United Nations in the fulfilment of its tasks".[103] A resolution drafted by Ceylon, Liberia and the United Arab Republic (Egypt–Syria) on behalf of the Afro-Asian group was adopted in a revised version on 21 February by nine votes to none, with the USSR and France abstaining. Its operative paragraphs introduced for the first time the use of force as a possible legitimate last resort:

> *The Security Council,*
>
> ...
>
> *Deeply concerned* at the grave repercussions of these crimes and the danger of widespread civil war and bloodshed in the Congo and the threat to international peace and security,

Noting the report of the Secretary-General's special representative (S/4691) dated February 12, 1961, bringing to light the development of a serious civil war situation and preparations therefore,

1. *Urges* that the United Nations take immediately all appropriate measures to prevent the occurrence of civil war in the Congo, including arrangements for cease-fires, the halting of all military operations, the prevention of clashes, and the use of force, if necessary, in the last resort;
2. *Urges* that measures be taken for the immediate withdrawal and evacuation from the Congo of all Belgian and other foreign military and paramilitary personnel and political advisers not under the United Nations command, and mercenaries;
3. *Calls upon* all states to take immediate and energetic measures to prevent the departure of such personnel for the Congo from their territories, and for the denial of transit and other facilities to them;[104]

Paragraph 4 called for an investigation into the circumstances of the killings and the punishment of the perpetrators, while paragraph 5 reaffirmed the earlier resolutions of the Council. As a concession to the USSR, no mention was made of the Secretary-General's responsibility as regards the implementation of the resolution. But in the understanding of the Western Council members paragraph 5 implicitly confirmed his continued authority.[105]

While Hammarskjöld welcomed the resolution immediately after its adoption "as giving a stronger and clearer framework for United Nations action", he also observed that "it does not provide a wider legal basis or new means for implementation".[106] Instead of being a breakthrough, clarifying the mandate, the resolution complicated matters even more and created another stalemate: both the Congolese government under Kasavubu and Mobutu (who were afraid of being implicated in the killing of Lumumba) and the secessionist Katanga administration under Tshombe vehemently resisted the idea that the United Nations would have the power to infringe on their authority, even by force of arms. Meanwhile, Western states showed no interest in putting pressure on Belgium to withdraw from Katanga. A vigorous diplomatic offensive undertaken by Hammarskjöld vis-à-vis the Congolese and Belgian governments as well as the Katangese secessionist leader Tshombe in the weeks following the resolution showed no results. Pressure on Hammarskjöld and the Secretariat mounted.[107]

The General Assembly discussed the Congo in several sessions from 7 March into April 1961. In response to attacks describing Hammarskjöld's futile efforts to implement the 21 February resolution as useless, he replied: "I would be very interested to know what alternatives there are to correspondence and talks when there is a question of pressing on people and authorities the necessity to implement resolutions. Is the alternative military means? If so, what troops would the Secretary-General have been able to use and with what legal authorization?"[108] Two draft resolutions introduced by the Afro-Asian group on 5 and 6 April 1961 condemned Belgium's failure to comply with the withdrawal of military personnel and political advisers as demanded by the Security Council resolution and called for further efforts towards reconciliation in the Congo as an alternative to a military solution. After several amendments the resolutions were adopted on 15 April. By a majority of votes the Assembly also adopted a third resolution to establish a commission of investigation into the death of Lumumba. A fourth and final statement by Hammarskjöld concluded the Assembly debates and ended as follows:

> On considering the whole question of the implementation of the resolutions, I think it would be appropriate to make a distinction between demands, authority, and means. I believe that all through the history of the Congo operation demands have gone far beyond authorization and authorization far beyond means. That is the only comment I would like to make on the new complaints.[109]

In July 1961 President Kennedy tried to intervene directly, mainly to satisfy domestic critics who claimed that his lenience towards newly independent Africa enhanced Communist influence. Concerned that Antoine Gizenga, who was suspected of representing Soviet interests,[110] would be elected as Prime Minister of Congo, Kennedy demanded that the United Nations should prevent Gizenga from taking office. If not, the United States and other Western powers might withdraw their support from the United Nations.[111] Hammarskjöld dismissed this threat. Despite slow progress, by early August 1961 the defunct Congolese parliament had reconstituted and achieved a modus operandi. It included the previously marginalised Lumumba faction in higher offices, with Antoine Gizenga as the first Deputy Prime Minister, and re-established a constitutional central government of the Republic of the Congo under President Kasavubu and Prime Minister Cyrille Adoula. But the continued presence of the Belgian military and hundreds of mercenaries in Katanga remained an unresolved issue and had even gained in number and influence. The mounting frustrations over the standstill and the lack of any progress in finding solutions as regards the withdrawal of foreign forces from Katanga finally turned into more desperate efforts to force the foreign collaborators out. On 24 August, President Kasavubu followed a proposal by Hammarskjöld and issued an ordinance for the immediate expulsion of all non-Congolese officers and mercenaries in the Katanga forces who had not entered into a contractual engagement with the central government. On the same day Prime Minister Adoula formally requested United Nations assistance in the execution of the ordinance. This provided legal authority for United Nations action within the Congo in accordance with the evacuation provision of the Security Council's February 21 resolution.[112]

When a final effort failed to bring Tshombe under United Nations protection to Léopoldville for a meeting with Adoula, Blue Helmets mounted a surprise attack under the code name Operation Rumpunch on the instruction of the Secretary-General's local representative in Katanga, Conor Cruise O'Brien.[113] In the early hours of 28 August, they occupied strategic key points in Elisabethville and other parts of Katanga to seize and repatriate Belgian officers and mercenaries. But instead of bringing the operation to its end, the forces withdrew assuming that the Belgian diplomats on the ground would ensure that the process would be completed as they had promised. When realising the mistake and being confronted with the subsequent radical and swift reinforcement of the "ultra" faction in the white presence in Katanga, the local ONUC officials in leading positions "proceeded to develop a plan for action which went considerably beyond the scope of the authority given them from Headquarters".[114] But unlike Rumpunch, Operation Morthor on 13 September 1961 did meet a prepared response from the regrouped forces in Katanga.

In the meantime, Hammarskjöld had accepted an invitation by Prime Minister Adoula on 10 September to visit Léopoldville before the opening of the United Nations General Assembly's annual session. Aware of the irritations created among Western member states by Operation Rumpunch, he had decided at short notice to return to the Congo for further direct negotiations with Tshombe. An exchange of cables prior to Operation Morthor suggests that the Secretary-General was involved in discussions preceding the second military intervention. Cables published by *The Guardian*[115] show that he had consulted his legal adviser, Oscar Schachter, who on 7 September 1961 warned strongly against such an engagement as "violation of the ban against intervention in domestic political conflicts".[116] But on 10 September 1961 Hammarskjöld cabled to Sture Linnér that "the speed of developments and the stage reached means that short of a change for the better in Katanga we are beyond the point of no return".[117] There seem to exist sufficient indications that he was involved in a discussion about whether a military presence by the United Nations might be instrumental in reversing the secession of Katanga.

Documents on Irish foreign policy for the years 1957 to 1961 were made accessible in November 2018. They include a letter of 18 September 1961 from Freddie Boland, then Irish permanent representative to the United Nations. In this he revealed that on asking Ralph Bunche whether the Secretary-General had ordered the attack, Bunche had replied: "Well, not exactly ordered—but authorised."[118]

It is not far-fetched to conclude that the military operations "were seen as a sacrifice of Western economic interests ... in return for Soviet support of a negotiated end to the civil war".[119] As O'Brien observed: "When Katanga is hurt, money screams, and money has powerful lungs ... Hammarskjöld was subjected to the most intense pressure, both psychological and diplomatic, to draw back from what the UN had undertaken—which was in fact the ending of the secession of Katanga by the use of force."[120]

Unable to obtain further guidelines from the Security Council on how to position the United Nations force in the midst of the local conflicts, the Secretary-General continued seeking to achieve the defined goals—withdrawal of Belgian troops and the reintegration of Katanga into the territory of the Congo. Beginning with his first efforts to clarify the mandate, Hammarskjöld stressed time and again—and then for the last time in a letter to Tshombe on 16 September 1961—that "the solution of the problem of the Congo lies in the hands of the Congolese people themselves without any interference from outside".[121] This was certainly more of an abstract reiteration of a noble-sounding principle rather than a reflection of reality. After all, the United Nations had already intervened through its mandate and its presence, though it had also explicitly declared that this intervention should not be seen as interference in the country's internal affairs.

On 17 September, Dag Hammarskjöld and 15 other members of his entourage and crew left Léopoldville on board a DC-6 on a flight that was considered risky. Hammarskjöld was to meet Tshombe in the Northern Rhodesian mining town of Ndola to negotiate in person an end to the Katanga secession.

> He refused to have O'Brien along, on the grounds that O'Brien had become part of the problem. What he wanted to do was, first of all, get Tshombe to order a cease-fire—which I think would have been easy to do; and then, if possible, to persuade Tshombe to come back to Leopoldville in his aircraft to have a grand Congolese reconciliation.[122]

The meeting never took place: the plane crashed when approaching the Ndola airport on the night of 17/18 September—nine months to the day after the execution of Patrice Lumumba. Diplomatic communications suggest that Hammarskjöld's plan could have been to offer a federalist solution to return the Katanga province in a semi-autonomous way to the national territory of the Congo, with Tshombe being appointed to a high-ranking position.[123] Already alarmed by the two failed military operations of the ONUC forces, Western interests were worried about losing firm control over the natural resources in the province. After all, "the death of Hammarskjöld took place in the context of intense competition among Western mining companies for access to Katanga, and had very little to do with the rivalry between East and West".[124] For Hammarskjöld, on the other hand, a solution to the conflict would have been a fitting end to his career at the helm of the organisation.

> While much had been achieved in the Hammarskjöld years, in the end the incumbent and some Council members were in open confrontation. Hammarskjöld had realized that his effectiveness and usefulness for the organization was being questioned, which discouraged him from running for a third term. Urquhart recounts that the Secretary-General had plans to resign as soon as the Congo question was resolved, and that he had told the Tunisian representative Mongi Slim with whom he had also worked in the Security Council, that the trip to Ndola would be his last personal mission.[125]

While speculation about the cause of the crash continues, the United Nations has since 2014 initiated new investigations. These are presented in detail in the following chapter. While the verdict is pending, "it is interesting to note that almost all of the major secret services in the world are at least suspects in one or another theory. In retrospect, Hammarskjöld's death becomes singular evidence of the Secretary-General's independence."[126]

Results and Lessons

In "summing up" towards the end of 1960, a journalist presented a well-informed and instructive balance sheet of the mixed results of the United Nations operation.[127] Of the five aims identified, the first—to expel Belgian troops from the Congo—was originally achieved. But it failed to do the same for those seconded to the army in Katanga. The second aim—of military assistance to the government, in order to maintain a pacification line between Katanga and the rest of the Congolese territory—was partially achieved. But the third aim—to restore the unity of the Congo—could hardly be achieved as long as the United Nations force was restricted to a purely "non-intervention" role. The contradiction was obvious from the start and reflected the antagonistic interests among the influential member states on whom the mandate depended. The fourth aim—of technical assistance in support of a functioning government—was considered perhaps the biggest achievement, at the time before the ultimate collapse of this government. But, as we have shown, by August 1961 a new government coalition had indeed been established and stability of a sort regained. The fifth aim—to keep the Cold War out of Africa—was obviously not fully achieved. As the Congo operation documents, the Cold War motivated efforts to influence any form of mandate and its implementation.

Hammarskjöld was fully aware of this fundamental obstacle, with which he constantly battled. In his last words to the staff, he once again reiterated the necessary autonomy of the Secretariat from the direct influence of member states as one of his fundamental principles. When the Secretariat, as he stated, "is regarded as truly international, and its individual members as owing no allegiance to any national government", then it "may develop as an instrument for the preservation of peace and security of increasing significance and responsibilities".[128] As he often stressed, the Charter "has committed the Organization to the furtherance of self-determination, self-government, and independence".[129] He also insisted that the fundamental principles, as laid down in the Charter, were of special significance for the practical work of the organisation "in relation to countries under colonial rule or in other ways under foreign domination. The General Assembly has translated the principles into action intended to establish through self-determination a free and independent life as sovereign states for peoples who have expressed in democratic forms their wish for such a status."[130]

It does not seem as if there is any convincing evidence to substantiate the claim that Hammarskjöld willingly promoted a Western imperialist agenda. If anything, the evidence suggests that, then as now, the hegemonic powers in our world sought to influence global policies above all in their own interests. Given the ambiguity of the Congo mandate, which was supposed to guide the ONUC mission, the space it provided for differing interpretations was both an advantage and a disadvantage. It failed to set out a clear frame of reference and left too many important aspects unclarified. This in turn increased the range of individual decisions and ways of handling matters. An approach that could be seen in a positive sense as flexible was at risk of being criticised as arbitrary or partisan. The collision of the two blocs at the height of the Cold War over the interests they had in the Congo turned the mission at times into a battlefield for securing or seeking advantages.

What remained was unfinished business the Secretary-General had left behind:

Hammarskjöld was certainly pro-Western but did not always go along with the United States, particularly when he determined (or was forced to see) that its goals were not conducive to overall international security (as he saw it). Yet Hammarskjöld was also a diplomat extraordinaire, and had he lived longer the crisis might have ended sooner or more peacefully. A major problem with his legacy is that his imprint on ONUC was so subtly managed and dependent on his personal relationships that it was impossible for others to follow. He was not supposed to die, and his untimely death threw into jeopardy all he had carefully crafted and managed in the Congo.[131]

The complicated mix of domestic political rivalries, external influence by other states, an unclear framework for the mandated intervention and personality clashes ended not only in deadly consequences for Lumumba. But while Hammarskjöld and the United Nations failed to end the conflict in the Congo, the intervention at least managed to prevent further escalation which might have provoked a much larger inter-state military battle for the control of geostrategic resources: "Whatever its failings, the UN remained the last best chance of keeping the Cold War at bay in the Congo."[132] Put differently: "The Congo crisis could easily have provoked armed conflicts in other parts of Africa, even led to a world war. It was Dag Hammarskjöld and no one else who prevented that."[133] On the other hand, one should be careful not to over-emphasise the impact and influence of an individual limited in the scope of his actions by the political environment in which his office was forced to operate: "One can speculate that the Congo drama might have turned out quite differently if Hammarskjold had not died ..., but evidence suggests that the outcome depended less on the personality of the Secretary-General than on the interplay of external and Congolese interests."[134]

This is a sobering but necessary reminder that one should not expect a Secretary-General to achieve miracles in the midst of a polarised world. It also points to the fact that while persons and personalities matter, the decisive factors determining the scope for success ultimately lie outside the direct influence of an individual and can only be used favourably depending on an individual's skill and ability to accommodate differing interests. After all, "The Secretary-General was never given authority to impose a political solution on the Congo."[135] A mandate that remains as open and unspecific as the one for the first Congo mission of the United Nations is potentially a recipe for failure, if not disaster. Instead of blaming Hammarskjöld, one should rather wonder at how much he was able to make out of it. While of late it seems *en vogue* to be harshly critical of Hammarskjöld's role, such conclusions seem as unjustified as those praise songs that award him the status of a hero.

Concluding Observations

Several issues raised in this case study seem of continuing relevance. The dynamics in the unfolding crisis of the Congo invite a few final observations. With foresight, Hammarskjöld commented in an internal communication as early as 19 July 1960:

> Congo operation is likely to go far beyond Suez story in all directions. If we succeed and if Seco [Security Council] accepts lines and philosophy developed in my report ... it will probably mean the opening of a new and decisive chapter in the history of under-developed countries and the UN. For the first time we come to grips with the realities of post-colonial era, and I hope that we will not fail.[136]

Hammarskjöld's concerns were certainly not far-fetched. As an observer said, the Congo "was simultaneously a hotbed of inter-African intrigue, a playground for the superpowers and a turning point in the decolonization process".[137] Like the Suez crisis, the situation prompted some strategic positioning by the influential member states. The US, while immediately engaging with a massive presence of the CIA on the ground, preferred not to involve itself too much in the peacekeeping mission. Rather, it responded to appeals for help by the Congolese government, "which it hoped would obviate any Congolese request for Soviet military assistance".[138] Washington's primary aim was to replace the Belgian presence by that of the United Nations and "replicate the 1956 Suez mission, when a multi-country UN coalition had successfully restored order" by forcing Israel out of Egypt: "This was the essence of containment: the United States would remain on the sidelines, but so too would the Soviet Union."[139]

In the course of events, this turned out to be wishful thinking, while Hammarskjöld understood and executed his office more as a General than as a Secretary. Claiming to be a proactive guardian of the Charter, he took the initiative when the Security Council was reluctant to act. It is very likely that a mandate would have not been adopted if it had not been for his personal initiative. This brings to the fore the relevant role a Secretary-General is able to play if he or she is willing. Not by coincidence, ever since Hammarskjöld's terms in office, the role of his successors has often been measured against his performance. This alerts us to the need to define the interaction between the member states and the Secretariat. In interpreting and executing the mandate, Hammarskjöld claimed he was jealously guarding the independent role of the Secretariat.

But the relative autonomy of such proactive leadership, which is able and willing to take responsibility, not only strengthens but also potentially weakens operations. After all, the implementation of the mandate thereby becomes dependent to a large extent upon a single person. Hammarskjöld used a new instrument by establishing an Advisory Board and the function of special representatives to expand the UN's operational scope and his authority. But this created new vulnerabilities. The execution of the mandate became the subject of interpretations not only by the member states, but also by a circle of persons (dubbed the "Congo Club") in the Secretariat and on the ground. Their personalities and loyalties became an important secondary factor and led to clashes and decisions with at times dramatic consequences: "For these UN senior officials, Lumumba's nationalism was a challenge because it was based on an exclusive concept of sovereignty that defied the notion of the UN as an organization superior to state authority."[140]

On the other hand, Hammarskjöld tried to remain in command of the execution of the mandate and, in doing so, did not allow member states to advance interpretations that would deviate from his understanding of the ONUC operations. For Hammarskjöld it would have been inconceivable to delegate parts of a mandate to forces outside his command and control, such as NATO or any other partisan organisation or states. Along with sole responsibility for the operations, the internal structures created in the Secretariat allowed for very quick communication and operationalised actions. Within not much more than a single day, the adoption of the mandate was followed by the appearance of the first contingents of Blue Helmets in the Congo. As a consequence of Hammarskjöld's hands-on approach, the Secretariat was hardly affected by bureaucratic red tape and was able to act without delays.

Being confronted with increased clashes of geostrategic interests between the Western states and the Soviet alliance over the Congo, Hammarskjöld resorted to and relied upon close cooperation with the growing number of member states from the Afro-Asian group. Resolutions were introduced mainly through them, which made it more difficult for any of the two blocs to simply object. Giving weight to the newly independent countries, Hammarskjöld in return received a lot of trust and support from leaders of these states. When he was confronted with massive criticism from any of the two competing power blocs, the Afro-Asian group remained to a large extent loyal to the Secretary-General even when they had serious concerns and different views on particular subjects. Similarly, in an effort to reduce dependence on the veto powers Hammarskjöld sought to find new avenues to strengthen his mandate, by resorting to the General Assembly instead of exclusively relying upon the Security Council. The power and impact of such resolutions should not be neglected.[141]

But, as we have seen, the international context within which the Congo mission had to be executed created insurmountable challenges. During the debate in the General Assembly in March and April 1961, Hammarskjöld summed up the limitations of a mandate that had to reconcile potentially antagonistic interests within the "first UN" (for example the member states), while delegating its execution to the "second UN" (for example the Secretary-General and the Secretariat). These limitations of the organisation have remained a problem until now:

> It has been said that the United Nations operation in the Congo is disappointing or even a failure. It seems reasonable to ask those who say so whether the reason for their disappointment is that the Organization has done anything less than it could do, or that elements beyond the control of the Organization have created difficulties which at the present stage of its development are insuperable for the instrument for international cooperation which Members have created in the United Nations, even when that instrument is strained to its utmost capacity. One can blame a mountain climber for his failure to reach the summit when his road has been blocked by an avalanche, but to do so is an irresponsible play on words.[142]

One of Hammarskjöld's self-declared aims was "to keep the Cold War in its sharper forms out of Africa".[143] This was like navigating between Scylla and Charybdis, and it was further complicated by the Security Council's authorisation of ONUC in a resolution that lacked any clear and concrete guidance. While this provided space for manoeuvring—at times the vagueness was deliberately used by Hammarskjöld—it carried the risk that, in the absence of clarity, parties whose own interests were involved would criticise whatever the Secretariat did. Evidence of unfortunate, even disastrous, interplay between members of the "Congo Club" and their individual interactions with local counterparts shows that the ONUC mission was vulnerable because it depended on individual decisions that were at times guided by personal preferences, limitations, prejudices and incompetence.

The Western powers, seeking to influence Hammarskjöld's policies, put as much pressure on his office as the Soviet Union did, though in different ways. After an initial brief period of support, he faced suspicions and criticisms from them for almost every decision he made. All were eager to force him to give into what they considered was in their interest. In an attempt to escape these efforts to hijack the United Nations' role and derail its policies, he sought the cooperation of as many states as possible from the Non-Aligned Movement. Egypt (Nasser), Ghana (Nkrumah), Guinea (Touré), India (Nehru) and Tunisia (Bourguiba) became important participants and at times even allies in visibly involving the "Third World" in international affairs and peacekeeping efforts. During Hammarskjöld's time in office, and especially from the start of the engagement in the Congo, the United Nations became a midwife for the concerted efforts of newly independent states guided by a "Southern" perspective. Importantly, "the characterisation of the Congo exclusively as a Cold War struggle tends to flatten the distinction between the intersecting levels of the crisis in which the dynamic agency of the UN and Third World actors comes into focus".[144]

This chapter has largely neglected the civilian operations by ONUC. But the link between the technical and the political-diplomatic and military aspects of ONUC adds another dimension that cannot be ignored. The Soviet Union had initially "evidenced little or no interest in the development activities of the UN".[145] This changed from the late 1950s with the emergence of newly independent states on the world stage and the increasingly relevant strategic role of the United Nations in their administrative support. At the time of the Congo crisis, the East–West dynamic penetrated global interactions to an extent that made any kind of neutrality in such assistance obsolete. ONUC's civilian operations, therefore, confirmed in practice a Western bias, exacerbated by the fact that only very few staff involved came from countries affiliated to the Eastern bloc.

> On several occasions, official spokesmen have praised the UN for keeping the cold war out of the Congo, and in their more candid moments they have substituted "communism" for the "cold war." ONUC's Civilian Operations have contributed to this result. State-preserving and state-building are tasks which have very wide political ramifications; the external actors involved in giving assistance cannot help but influence the future political orientation of the recipient. Surely this has been the case in the Congo. While ONUC's Civilian Operations may not have done much to advance the goals of democracy, they certainly have done nothing to advance the goals of communism and their influence has been basically Western.[146]

But the author of this quotation also concedes that "there can be no question that the UN has made a significant contribution to decolonization by its activities in this instance".[147]

On balance, the Congo mission is a sobering but necessary reminder that we should not expect a Secretary-General and the global governance agency which he heads to operate aloof from its fundamental contradictions or to achieve miracles in a polarised world. It reminds us too that while persons and personalities matter, the decisive factors for success may ultimately lie beyond the individual's direct influence. Whether he or she can take advantage of certain emerging constellations of forces will depend on his or her skills and abilities to accommodate conflicting interests. But despite the mixed record, it is worth considering the questions (and suggested answers) raised in the following quotation:

> What would have happened to the Congo without the United Nations? With the UN it at least survived. In the Congo the UN indeed played out three of its roles in Africa. At times the UN was a collective imperial power—as its sins of both omission and commission cost Patrice Lumumba his life. The UN in the Congo was also Africa's partner in development—trying to safeguard the pre-conditions of national integrity and political stability for the fragile Congo. But the UN was also an ally of Africa's liberation as it tried to prevent new forms of re-colonization of the Congo by Belgians and others.[148]

7

DEATH AT NDOLA

The way
You shall follow it.
Success,
You shall forget it.
The cup,
You shall empty it.
The pain,
You shall conceal it.
The answer,
You shall learn it.
The end,
You shall endure it.[1]

On 17 September 1961, NBC aired a special television feature by Pauline Frederick, in which she "predicted that Hammarskjöld would be ousted from his job, saying, metaphorically, that the 'peacemaker', as she labeled him, would be 'sacrificed'".[2] As Frederick stressed afterwards, she did not suggest that he would be assassinated. But almost at the same time as the broadcast, Hammarskjöld and 15 others[3] were on board a DC-6B plane called *Albertina* (SE-BDY). It crashed upon approaching the airport of the mining town Ndola, near the border of the Congo and Katanga province, in what was then Northern Rhodesia (now Zambia). This trip, part of the "Congo disaster"[4] unfolding since mid-1960, was the result of an ad hoc decision and the culmination of mediation efforts to seek a solution to the Katanga secession. The Secretary-General was on his way to meet Moise Tshombe, the Katangan leader, but never arrived. "In a sense, Hammarskjöld's unswerving high principles and his determined search for peaceful solutions contributed to his death. A different Secretary-General, faced with the Katangan crisis in September 1961, might have found an easier option than flying, exhausted, to a small town in central Africa to negotiate with an enemy of the United Nations."[5]

After several initial investigations, the murky circumstances surrounding the crash remained for decades out of the public limelight and only occasionally provoked interest through the publication of new reports—often on the sensational side and close to conspiracy theories.[6] More recently, however, new official investigations by the United Nations have been triggered by the credible revelations of a meticulously researched study. It published disturbing evidence half a century after the crash.[7] A subsequent private initiative, campaigning for a reopening of the case, finally resulted in new official investigations by the United Nations. This chapter presents an overview of events, the steps towards the new investigations, and the interim results until the end of 2018.[8]

Katanga and the Plane Crash

Dag Hammarskjöld, together with all but one of his companions, died in the wreckage of the *Albertina* on the night of 17/18 September 1961. Most passengers were burnt beyond recognition in the blaze of the debris, though Hammarskjöld's body was found almost undamaged, reportedly leaning against an anthill.[9] As photos taken of the body revealed, an ace of spades was stuck in his shirt collar.[10] The bodyguard Harold Julien was the only survivor. He died six days later in a local hospital. Evidence suggests that he could have been saved if treated properly.

Suspicions were immediately aroused that there might have been foul play. Not only did investigative journalists already point in this direction.[11] Even former US President Harry S. Truman was quoted in the *New York Times* of 20 September 1961[12] as stating: "Dag Hammarskjöld was on the point of getting something done when they killed him. Notice that I said 'When they killed him.'" Pressed for a further explanation, he maintained: "That's all I've got to say on the matter. Draw your own conclusions."

The natural resources of the Congo, and in particular Katanga, were then as now one of the country's major attractions. By far the most important were rich deposits of uranium in Katanga's Shinkolobwe mine. They had fuelled since the 1940s the US nuclear programme in the Cold War arms race.

Shinkolobwe supplied the material for the atomic bombs dropped at Hiroshima and Nagasaki, and remained of utmost importance.[13] Diamonds and other precious deposits added to the attraction: "the Congo's resources, including its uranium, put the newly independent nation at the very heart of Cold War concerns".[14] The geostrategic interests of various states, the agendas of mining companies, the security obsessions of racist minority regimes in the neighbouring settler colonies seeking formal ties if not a merger with Katanga,[15] and the activities of intelligence agents, mercenaries and all sorts of dubious "entrepreneurs", together created a toxic situation.

As we have seen, the role of the United Nations and its Secretary-General was a difficult if not impossible mission and has drawn controversial assessments. But evidence seems to suggest that Hammarskjöld was, despite accusations, not the wilful instrument of the Western hegemonic powers. Seeking to meet the leader of the Katangan secessionist movement on "neutral ground" was yet another effort to negotiate an end to the conflict after the botched attempts of Blue Helmet military interventions.

Several parties could have been interested in preventing such a meeting—if not the removal of the Secretary-General from his office. The Western governments were aware of Hammarskjöld's role in proactively seeking an end to the secession of Katanga, and their strong disapproval was conveyed to him.[16] Dismissing criticism by the US, Hammarskjöld cabled on 15 September 1961 to Ralph Bunche, who played a somewhat unfortunate role in the Congo dealings:

> It is better for the UN to lose the support of the US because it is faithful to law and principles than to survive as an agent whose activities are geared to political purposes never avowed or laid down by the major organs of the UN ... Generally speaking, I have one advice and that is that the major powers do not react until they know the facts and, further, that they do remember that they are most likely to keep their positions if they respect principles than if they expect others to break them on their behalf or on behalf of the Welenskys.[17]

Sir Roy Welensky, then Prime Minister of the Federation created by Britain in 1953 between Northern and Southern Rhodesia and Nyasaland (nowadays Zambia, Zimbabwe and Malawi respectively), was a strong ally of Tshombe and a declared opponent of Hammarskjöld's role in the decolonisation processes in Africa. In his memoirs, Welensky deals at some length with the plane crash and expresses the hope that

> history will say that it was a grim, sad, wasteful affair, but that we were utterly guiltless of the reckless and cruel accusations which were hurled at us. I accept

the Federal Commission's careful study and firm rejection of eleven suggested causes of the accident ... and I commend the forbearance and clarity with which they concluded that the cause was a pilot error, "a visual descending procedure in which the aircraft was brought too low". I resent the way in which the UN Commission first, having admitted that it found no evidence of sabotage, or of ground or air attack, then states that none of these possibilities can be excluded; and second, having considered the Federal Commission's scrupulous and candid conclusion, says that it "has found no indication that this was the probable cause of the crash".[18]

In Welensky's version, "an unidentified aircraft flew over the airfield and disappeared, heading west; there was not the slightest indication that this was Mr. Hammarskjöld's aircraft, nor had we any reason to assume that it was".[19] Indeed? After all, the only reason for all the diplomats, secret agents, mercenaries, officials and others to gather on the ground was to wait for the arrival of Dag Hammarskjöld. After an announcement that the landing procedure had begun, radio contact with the *Albertina* ended abruptly. The plane disappeared. Later on, the lights at the landing strip were simply switched off and people went to sleep. "What was scandalous was that the British authorities in Ndola should have found it [the wreckage] instantly. They actually saw the flash, but they didn't like Hammarskjöld, they didn't like the UN, and they just closed down. They didn't even look for the wreckage."[20]

A search mission was only initiated the next morning and the ground was combed in the opposite direction to the assumed approach. The wreckage was officially discovered only in the afternoon. But several eyewitnesses testified later that the crash site had already been cordoned off and access to it denied early in the morning.[21] As a British journalist observed: "Flying in a chartered Cessna aircraft at 9 am over the bush I saw a long narrow rift in the trees. Police were already moving about the clearing among the grey ash of the wreckage."[22]

Several inquiries presented their versions of what happened within months of the event. An air accident investigation by the Rhodesian Federal Department of Civil Aviation[23] concluded that pilot error was a possibility, but was unable to rule out the "willful act of some person or persons unknown which might have forced the aircraft to descend or collide with the trees".[24] In contrast to this initial investigation, a subsequent Rhodesian Commission of Inquiry presented a report in February 1962 which identified pilot error as the sole reason for the crash.[25] It based its findings on the original evidence compiled by the Board of Investigation, which had ignored numerous local eyewitnesses, describing them as unreliable and not trustworthy.[26] The inquiry by a

United Nations Commission, reporting in April 1962, despite acknowledging any lack of evidence, did not exclude sabotage or attack in the air as possible causes of the fatal crash. "It noted that the Rhodesian inquiry, by eliminating to its satisfaction other possible causes, had reached the conclusion that the probable cause of the crash was pilot error. The Commission, while it cannot exclude this possibility, has found no indication that this was the probable cause of the crash."[27]

It ended on a critical note:

> although SE-BDY crashed 9.5 miles from the airfield on which eighteen military aircraft capable of carrying out an air search were stationed, the wreckage was located by the Rhodesian authorities only 15 hours after the crash and more than 9 hours after first light on 18 September 1961 ... Undue weight appeared to be attached to the groundless impression that the Secretary-General had changed his mind after flying over Ndola and decided to land at another airport without informing the Ndola tower. Had that degree of diligence been shown which might have been expected in the circumstances, it is possible that the crash could have been discovered at an earlier hour and Sgt. Julien's chances of survival materially improved. Had he survived, not only would one life have been saved but there would have existed a possible source of direct knowledge of the conditions and circumstances surrounding the tragedy.[28]

Having given effect to the United Nations Commission of Inquiry by Resolution 1628(XVI) of 26 October 1961,[29] the General Assembly acknowledged the report by Resolution 1759(XVII) of 26 October 1962. Notably, it requested the Secretary-General "to inform the General Assembly of any new evidence which may come to his attention",[30] hereby indicating the wish to remain apprised of the matter in case new insights came to light justifying further investigations.

New Investigations

Another report was commissioned in 1992 by the Swedish government and undertaken by a diplomat who at the time of the plane crash had been the Swedish consul-general in Léopoldville. The investigation was in response to claims that a Belgian jet pilot had confessed to having shot down the *Albertina* when approaching Ndola.[31] The report dismissed the allegations and considered pilot error as the likely cause, but accused the officials on the ground of having deliberately delayed the search and rescue operation.

Finally, fifty years after Ndola, Susan Williams—a historian at the Institute for Commonwealth Studies/School for Advanced Study at the University of

London, who had grown up in Zambia—presented a bombshell with her book *Who Killed Hammarskjöld?* While offering no conclusive answers, the evidence it presented fully justified the question asked in the title. Widely reported in the public media, the book soon managed to create new interest in the case.

Following the book's publication, fresh inquiries took place. The first was conducted by an independent international commission of jurists, which produced a report in 2013; the second—as a direct consequence of the first— by a panel of experts set up by United Nations Secretary-General Ban Ki-moon. After verifying the independent inquiry, it reported back in 2015. In 2017, an Eminent Person was tasked with further investigations as a follow-up. His mandate has since been extended. The chronology of events is listed online by the Dag Hammarskjöld Library at the United Nations in New York, with links to the relevant reports.[32] The United Nations Association Westminster Branch in London has preserved information relating to the first inquiry, which is available online;[33] it has also provided updates on developments since 2014 on a dedicated website.[34] The initiatives following *Who Killed Hammarskjöld?* and their results are presented here.

The Hammarskjöld Commission

The revelations in *Who Killed Hammarskjöld?* motivated Lord Lea of Crondall, who had not known Susan Williams before, to establish in early 2012 an Enabling Committee. This was transformed into the Hammarskjöld Inquiry Trust with the intention of facilitating further credible investigations into the circumstances of the crash. The eight members included, apart from Lord Lea, who was the chairperson, Susan Williams, the former Archbishop of the Church of Sweden, K.G. Hammar, the former Secretary-General of the Commonwealth, Chief Emeka Anyaoku, and the barrister Lord Marks of Henley-on-Thames. Other members were the former director of the Dag Hammarskjöld Institute of Peace and current Vice-Chancellor of the Copperbelt University in Kitwe, Naison Ngoma, the Norwegian researcher Hans Kristian Simensen, and the author of this book.

By mid-2012, the group had appointed four distinguished commissioners, willing to serve *pro bono* to investigate further the evidence collected in Susan Williams's book. These were Sir Stephen Sedley as chairperson, a former British High Court judge and Lord Justice of Appeal and a judge of the European Court of Human Rights; the Swedish Ambassador Hans Corell, previously Under-Secretary-General for Legal Affairs and the legal counsel of the United Nations; Justice Richard Goldstone, who had served at the Constitutional Court of South Africa and as first chief prosecutor of the United Nations International Criminal Tribunals for the former Yugoslavia and Rwanda; and Justice Wilhelmina Thomassen, who was a judge at the European Court of Human Rights and of the Supreme Court of the Netherlands before that. Several experts provided their services free of charge to the commission, which was supported by a full-time secretary, the only person remunerated.[35]

The commission's remit was to review the evidence that was available in order to determine whether there was a case for reopening the UN Inquiry of 1961–2. If the evidence was found to warrant reopening the UN Inquiry, it would be presented to the United Nations, pursuant to General Assembly Resolution 1759 (XVII). As a point of departure, the commission critically examined the findings of the report by the original United Nations Commission, and came to the following conclusion:

> When the UN Commission ... reported that it "did not consider it necessary to duplicate all the work already done", we respectfully think that it may have been surrendering part of its judgment to a less reliable predecessor. It appears, among other things, to have adopted the Rhodesian Commission's view that those African witnesses who claimed to have seen other aircraft in the vicinity of the DC6 were seeking, for nationalist reasons, to embarrass or discredit the Federal government.[36]

It further concluded that the Rhodesian investigation had

> led the UN Commission to underrate or marginalise the evidence of the sole first-hand witness of the disaster, Sgt. Julien ... The initial Board of Investigation appears to have been persuaded by the evidence of the surgeon who had overall but not clinical responsibility for Julien's care that Julien throughout his time in hospital was not coherent, so that nothing he said was reliable ... Other doctors and nurses gave a different picture, but were not taken seriously ... One apparent consequence was that, out of 27 possible witnesses who were able to testify about Julien, the Rhodesian Commission heard 8, and the UN Commission 5 of these 8.[37]

Archival searches were undertaken in Belgium, Sweden, the UK and the US. Operating on a shoestring budget, two of the commissioners visited Ndola in May 2013 and interviewed several of the eyewitnesses still alive. In Ndola, the commission "received eyewitness testimony which was not heard by any of the three initial inquiries. Most of these African witnesses had believed in 1961 that they would not be listened to, and indeed might get into trouble, if they told the Rhodesian authorities what they had seen. Some knew nothing of any inquiry."[38] All except two of the witnesses had not known each other, which gives additional credibility to their individual observations. Based on the accounts, the commission drew the conclusion that there was

> enough primary evidence that the plane was on fire when it crashed to call attention to the hypothesis that it was caused to descend by some internal or external damage sufficient to reduce the pilot's control ... Much of the evidence which supports this hypothesis is equally capable of supporting the alternative hypothesis—that the pilot was attempting to evade an attack or a threat of attack.[39]

After carefully weighing up all available evidence, the commission concluded:

> There is persuasive evidence that the aircraft was subjected to some form of attack or threat as it circled to land at Ndola, which was by then widely known to be its destination. Accepting, as we do, that there is—as the experts advise—no need for such an explanation to account for the crash and that it is capable of being fully explained as a controlled flight into terrain, we nevertheless consider that the possibility that the plane was in fact forced into its descent by some form of hostile action is supported by sufficient evidence to merit further inquiry.[40]

Sir Brian Unwin, who had been present at Ndola as the private secretary to Lord Alport, the British High Commissioner in Rhodesia, in a recorded interview with the commission, drew attention to the fact that two aircraft of the United States Air Force (USAF) were among those waiting for the *Albertina* to arrive. The commission quotes him as saying: "Those planes we understood had high powered communication equipment and it did occur to us to wonder later, whether there had been any contact between one or other of the two United States planes with Hammarskjold's aircraft, as they had, we understood, the capability to communicate with Hammarskjold's plane."[41]

The commission assumed that the presence of the USAF planes was part of the US National Security Agency's worldwide monitoring activities and that "it is highly likely that the entirety of the local and regional Ndola radio traffic ... was tracked and recorded by the NSA, and possibly also the CIA".[42] It considered these records as the most promising primary evidence, which could shed further light on what really happened: "any archived recording covering the last minutes of the *Albertina*, whether or not it corroborates a particular account or allegation, is likely to assist in explaining why the aircraft crashed".[43] A request under the Freedom of Information Act submitted to the National Security Archive at George Washington University was dismissed. According to the NSA's response, the documents were classified as "top secret" on national security grounds and therefore exempted from disclosure. An appeal has been lodged.

After asking if significant new evidence about Dag Hammarskjöld's death existed, the commission concluded: "Undoubtedly it does". It identified a golden thread in the maze of evidence but refused to speculate about the concrete motives or the actual initiators of the possible hostile aerial act. It maintained that the investigation into whether such an act had occurred and "whether it is considered to have caused the descent of the plane by direct damage or by harassment, or to have triggered some form of disabling harm to the plane, is ... capable of proof or disproof".[44]

The commission therefore felt that a follow-up by the United Nations would be appropriate. Such a decision was, however, purely at the authority and discretion of the member states and required a submission adopted by resolution in the General Assembly. The commission concluded that, far from obscuring the facts, this initiative "may have brought us somewhat closer to the truth about an event of global significance which deserves the attention both of history and justice".[45] Its report was publicly handed over to the Hammarskjöld Inquiry Trust at the Peace Palace in The Hague on 9 September 2013. The same day the United Nations Secretary-General in a press release thanked the commission and the trust and announced that "he would closely study the findings".[46]

United Nations Investigations

After legal experts in the Secretary-General's office had closely scrutinised the independent commission's report, Ban's decision was affirmative. On 21 March 2014 he shared the report with all member states with a note stating in no uncertain terms:

1. Pursuant to paragraph 3 of General Assembly resolution 1759(XVII), I have the duty to inform you that new evidence has come to my attention relating to the conditions and circumstances resulting in the tragic death of Dag Hammarskjöld and of the members of the party accompanying him.

    ...

5. Given the open verdict of the 1961–1962 United Nations Inquiry and given the possibility that the new evidence already in the possession of the Secretary-General may lead to a conclusive finding about the current theories of the causes of the crash of the former Secretary-General's plane, the General Assembly may wish to consider the following options:

(a) To establish an independent panel of experts, including forensic and ballistic experts, to examine the new evidence, to assess its probative value and to make recommendations to the General Assembly;

(b) To reopen the 1961–1962 Inquiry; or

(c) To establish a new inquiry.[47]

He also called on member states "to declassify any relevant records in their possession".[48] This initiative paved the way for turning the Secretary-General's recommendations into a draft resolution for adoption by the General Assembly. Across the world—from Australia to Zimbabwe—the media highlighted the issue in print, on the radio and on television. But until September 2014, the conservative alliance of parties in the Swedish government considered the matter a non-issue and rejected any need for further initiatives. "Sweden welcomes anything that can be done to shed further light on the plane crash," said the press secretary of Foreign Minister Carl Bildt, who held especially strong views, in reply to an enquiry by a journalist. "But we consider this primarily a matter for the United Nations."[49] While the Secretary-General's report was waiting to become an agenda item for the General Assembly deliberations, no proposal for a draft resolution along any of the lines suggested seemed in sight. However, on 14 September 2014, Sweden voted into power a new coalition government of the Social Democratic Party and the Green Party.[50] Within weeks it reversed the previous government's position—with a decisive impact on further developments. On 15 December 2014, Ambassador Per Thöresson of the Swedish Mission introduced a draft resolution to the General Assembly.[51] Supported by 20 other countries, it called for further investigations into Hammarskjöld's death and set out the following proposals: that the Secretary-General appoint an independent panel of experts to examine new information and to assess its probative value; that member states be encouraged to release any relevant records in their possession; and that the Secretary-General report on progress made to the General Assembly at its seventieth session.[52] Additional member states joined Sweden to co-sponsor the resolution, making 55 altogether. The resolution was adopted by the consensus of all 193 member states on 29 December 2014.[53] This was a dramatic development, which marked a profound shift in perceptions over the previous three years. There were still some people who attributed the crash to pilot error, along the lines of the Rhodesian Commission of Inquiry's report of 1962. But this was no longer the mainstream view: concerns about the crash were now regarded by many across the world as serious questions that required equally serious answers.

On 16 March 2015, Ban Ki-moon appointed a Panel of Experts to review information related to the crash and to evaluate its probative value. The panel was headed by Mohamed Chande Othman, the former Chief Justice of the United Republic of Tanzania.[54] The panel conducted its inquiry from April to June 2015, including a visit to Zambia to interview new witnesses. It also gathered additional new information from member states and other sources, including national and private archives in Belgium, Sweden and the UK. The panel's report was presented to the Secretary-General on 11 June 2015. In his letter of transmittal, Justice Othman said it was the panel's conclusion "that the final revelation of the whole truth ... would still require the United Nations, as a matter of continuity and priority, to further critically address remaining information gaps, including in the existence of classified material and information held by Member States".[55] On 2 July 2015, Ban forwarded the report to the General Assembly. In his letter, he summarised the findings. It had assigned moderate "probative value", he explained, to the following new information "relevant to the hypothesis of an aerial attack or other interference as a possible cause or causes of the crash":

(a) Nine new eyewitness accounts that they observed more than one aircraft in the air at the same time as SE-BDY made its approach to Ndola, and that any additional aircraft were jets, or that SE-BDY was on fire before it impacted the ground or that it was fired upon or otherwise actively engaged by other aircraft present;

(b) The claims by two persons regarding hearing alleged intercepts or reading transcripts of intercepts of radio transmissions relating to a possible aerial or ground attack on SE-BDY;

(c) Additional information that has emerged on the air capability of the provincial government of Katanga in 1961 and its use of foreign military and paramilitary personnel;

(d) The possibility that communications sent from the CX-52 cryptographic machine used by Mr. Hammarskjöld were intercepted;

(e) The possible role of crew fatigue as a contributing factor to the crash of SE-BDY under one or more of the hypotheses of the possible causes of the crash; and

(f) Additional information that calls into question the official account of the time of discovery of the crash site and the behaviour of various officials and local authorities.[56]

The Secretary-General stated that "the Panel ultimately found significant new information that it assessed as having sufficient probative value to further pursue aerial attack or other interference as a hypothesis". In his view, "a further inquiry or investigation would be necessary to finally establish the facts".[57]

On 13 November 2015 the permanent representative of the Swedish Mission, Ambassador Olof Skoog, circulated a draft resolution co-sponsored by 37 other countries (including Belgium). It followed up on the Secretary-General's recommendations by urging all member states to release any relevant records in their possession and requesting the Secretary-General to inform the General Assembly before the end of the ongoing seventieth session of any further progress.[58] On 19 November, the resolution was introduced by Skoog, now supported by 74 other states—including Belgium, France, Germany and Russia, but neither the UK nor the US. As he stated: "The contrast between what we know about Hammarskjöld's life and legacy—even his inner thoughts—on the one hand, and what we still don't know about the circumstances surrounding his death remains troubling."[59] The resolution was adopted unopposed.

On 17 August 2016 Ban Ki-moon complied with the resolution to report back to the General Assembly on the ongoing efforts to receive further information from the member states.[60] He attached as annexes to his statement the responses by several member states to the earlier call for documentation. These reveal to a large extent the continued uncooperative nature of the US and the UK. The US government, for example, which had been asked to search for records relating to United States Air Force (USAF) aircraft at Ndola airport on the crash night, stated that the USAF had conducted a search; but, surprisingly, it did not appear to have asked the State Department, National Security Agency, CIA or any other government department to do so. The UK government finally responded on 23 June 2016 to the request for documentation, circulated by Under-Secretary-General Miguel de Serpa Soares in November the year before. The Under-Secretary-General had specifically and clearly asked the UK government to state whether or not it had consulted MI5, MI6 and GCHQ (Government Communications Headquarters) for relevant records; however, the British response evaded the question. On the separate matter of redactions from files held by the UK national archives, the British government refused to release them, arguing that doing so would not provide anything of value; but it is impossible to verify this judgement without access to these redactions. In his note, Ban called on the forthcoming seventy-first General Assembly to reiterate its message to member states "to ensure that any relevant records that remain classified, more than 50 years after the fact, are declassified or otherwise made available for review by any eminent person or persons whom the Assembly may wish to entrust with this mandate. As I have previously noted, this may be our last chance to find the truth."[61]

The Secretary-General's appeal was once again followed by a draft resolution submitted by Sweden's permanent representative in the General Assembly. Adopted on 23 December 2016, it requested "the Secretary-General to appoint an eminent person to review the potential new information, including that which may be available from Member States, to assess its probative value, to determine the scope that any further inquiry or investigation should take and, if possible, to draw conclusions from the investigations already conducted".[62] In a follow-up, Secretary-General António Guterres appointed former Chief Justice Othman on 8 February 2017. On 24 July he presented his report to the Secretary-General, who circulated it on 5 September 2017 among the member states.

In his summary of the preliminary findings, the Eminent Person presented some new revelations, which justified continued efforts to come closer to what might have happened. Othman had received new information "which appears to establish that Rhodesian and United Kingdom authorities intercepted United Nations communications in the Congo". He also "received confirmation from the United States regarding the presence of its military assets in and around Ndola on that fatal flight". This included "between one and three Dakota aircraft", which "had sophisticated communications equipment which allowed them to intercept, transmit and receive communications over long distances".[63] This finally confirmed what had been suspected, and suggested that records of transmissions might indeed exist, though they have not been disclosed. Othman also managed to substantiate with strong probative value "that on or about 16 February 1961, three Fouga jets that had been purchased from France were delivered to Katanga by a United States commercial carrier, against objections of the Government of the United States". He also obtained other information of "Fouga jets having flown at night or from unpaved airfields in Katanga, both of which suggest that the pilots there were able to utilize the jet outside of its ordinary capabilities". He also received information "that at least one Dornier DO-28 aircraft appears to have been supplied on a commercial basis to Katanga from West Germany before the night of 17 to 18 September 1961 and that the aircraft may have been modified to be able to conduct aerial attacks and bombings during the day and night".[64] Further information indicated "that there may have been more airfields existing in and around Katanga at the relevant time than had originally been understood and that Katangan forces were apparently not limited to using airfields in Katanga".[65] This information finally put paid to the claims of those who dismissed suspicions that a second plane might have been interfering with the

Albertina when approaching Ndola. According to them, there wasn't any possibility of such interference because there weren't suitable planes or pilots in the vicinity. Othman was not able "to conclude exactly how many or which mercenary pilots may have been present in Katanga at the relevant time. However, it appears established that there were more than had been considered by the early inquiries."[66]

Othman also acknowledged new information indicating that "some Member States may have attempted to influence the early inquiries to find that pilot error was the cause of the crash", with the UK "having been provided with the 1961 Commission's report in draft before its issuance ... [and] having negotiated changes to the text".[67] As the document obtained disclosed further, "an attempt was made to influence the 1961 Commission to rule out sabotage or other malicious action as a probable cause or causes of the air crash".[68] Other new evidence reconfirmed that "the wreck was discovered at least some hours before"[69] and that "Rhodesian and United Kingdom authorities intercepted United Nations communications ... and may have shared the intelligence with the United States".[70]

The Eminent Person's report concluded "that there is likely to be much relevant material that remains undisclosed" and "that the continued non-disclosure of potentially relevant new information in the intelligence, security and defence archives of Member States constitutes the biggest barrier to understanding the full truth of the event".[71] Based on the new evidence collected, "an aerial attack on SE-BDY would have been possible using resources existing in the area at the time".[72]

> On balance, there is an ample sum of relevant eyewitness evidence that tends to establish that there was more than one aircraft in the air at the time SE-BDY made its approach to Ndola, that any aircraft present other than SE-BDY was a jet, that SE-BDY was on fire before it collided with the ground, and that SE-BDY may have been fired upon or otherwise actively engaged by one or more other aircraft. This evidence will need to be further considered as the record develops, and should be assessed against information from Member State intelligence, security and defence archives, which it is hoped will be forthcoming.[73]

This required "an unqualified, unreserved disclosure of relevant information that may exist but has so far been withheld".[74] Othman therefore recommended "that the burden of proof has now shifted to Member States to show that they have conducted a full review of records and archives in their custody or possession, including those that remain classified", and that relevant member states be requested to act accordingly by appointing "an independent and high-ranking official to conduct a dedicated internal review".[75]

In his letter accompanying the report, Secretary-General Guterres noted the Eminent Person's conclusion that

a further inquiry or investigation would be necessary to finally establish the facts and "that the information made available to the United Nations has been insufficient to come to conclusions about the cause or causes of the crash, and it seems likely that important additional information exists". I also note his related conclusion "that the burden of proof has now shifted to Member States to show that they have conducted a full review of records and archives in their custody or possession, including those that remain classified, for potentially relevant information". I therefore support the Eminent Person's recommendation that relevant Member States appoint an independent and high-ranking official to conduct a dedicated and internal review of their archives, in particular their intelligence, security and defence archives, to determine whether they hold relevant information.[76]

As before, the Swedish government took the initiative to follow up on this recommendation. A draft resolution circulated on 28 November 2017, co-sponsored by another 70 states (including again Belgium, France, Germany and Russia), was introduced in the General Assembly on 6 December 2017 and adopted without a vote on 24 December. It requested the Secretary-General to reappoint the Eminent Person; to ensure that the United Nations' own records and archives were reviewed for possible declassification of relevant information; and encouraged member states holding relevant information to appoint, as recommended, an independent and high-ranking official "to conduct a dedicated internal review of their intelligence, security and defence archives to determine whether relevant information exists, and to communicate a summary of the results to the Secretary-General before the end of the main part of the seventy-third session".[77] Complying with the resolution, Secretary-General Guterres announced the reappointment of Judge Othman in a statement of 27 March 2018.[78]

On 3 December 2018, Miguel de Serpa Soares, as Under-Secretary-General for Legal Affairs and United Nations legal counsel, presented an oral briefing based on an interim report by Judge Othman to the forty-fourth meeting of the seventy-third session of the General Assembly.[79] As Judge Othman reiterated, with his new assignment and the subsequent initiatives "the burden of proof has shifted to Member States to show that they have conducted a full review of all records and archives in their custody or possession ... for potentially relevant information".[80] After his reappointment, the Eminent Person asked nine member states to mandate high-ranking independent officials to identify any potentially relevant information. Belgium, Canada, France, Germany, Sweden and the United States subsequently complied with the request. The Russian Federation made no such appointment but indicated that its authorities undertook such a review. South Africa did not respond, despite numerous approaches. The United Kingdom responded that "it did not intend to appoint an independent and high-ranking official because all information of direct value to the investigation had been made available by the United Kingdom in previous years or had been released and is available publicly".[81] But as Othman commented: "the fact that certain Member States have not responded to repeated requests in 2018 to make such an appointment in line with resolution 72/252, or to engage with this process at all, has a crucial bearing on the success or failure of the full implementation of the above General Assembly resolution".[82] In June 2018, Othman also requested Angola, the DRC, Portugal, Zambia and Zimbabwe to appoint an independent person, since he considered it possible that they might also hold relevant information. The DRC and Zimbabwe have since then complied. The Eminent Person expects final written reports by 30 March 2019 and will submit his final report to the Secretary-General in mid-2019. As the Under-Secretary-General stressed during the briefing, the active participation of member states remains the most important factor. While the investigation and its conclusions are pending, Ambassador Irina Schoulgin Nyoni, on behalf of Sweden, delivered a statement at the briefing, welcoming the progress made. She ended with the appeal:

> Judge Othman has concluded that the burden of proof has shifted to Member States to show that we all have conducted full reviews of records and archives, including those that remain classified. We must all show beyond any uncertainty that we have done just that. We owe it to the families of those who perished 57 years ago and to this organization itself.
>
> We count on the full cooperation of all Member States, it is our shared responsibility to pursue the full truth in this matter.[83]

Mission Not Yet Accomplished

Despite all these efforts, there is still no conclusive evidence that the crash—either deliberately or by accident—was the result of external influence on the instruction or with the encouragement or at least knowledge of any of the parties who were following Hammarskjöld's attempt to end the Katangan secession. But those sceptical of the "pilot error" version had reasons to welcome the findings of the subsequent investigations, triggered by the initial private initiative following the revelations in *Who Killed Hammarskjöld?* After all, it is not farfetched to conclude that the military operations by the Blue Helmets "were considered as putting Western interests and those of the white settler regimes at risk".[84] As the Hammarskjöld Commission aptly said:

> by September 1961, a number of states, or state agencies, and major commercial enterprises had a stake in the secession of Katanga. In short, Belgium, the British and American security services, the Rhodesian Federation (together with its British supporters) and the Republic of South Africa had reasons not to welcome the prospect of a reunited and independent Congo which was the UN's policy and Dag Hammarskjöld's mission to bring about.[85]

Instead of jumping to conclusions, the commission merely pointed to the assumption that "the United Nations, deploying authority which the Commission does not possess, would be justified in reopening its 1961–2 inquiry for the initial purpose of confirming or refuting, from intercept records, the evidence indicating that the descent of the Secretary-General's plane was brought about by some form of attack or threat".[86] Despite several official investigative efforts since then, such verification has so far been denied by lack of access to any possibly existing information. The non-compliance of some of the member states with such investigations, notably the UK and the US, is of no comfort to those who continue to wonder what really happened that night. What could be "so toxic", asked an article in the *International New York Times*, "that those records must remain occluded today?"[87]

Interestingly, a close reading of some scholarly work published without a direct link to the current new efforts adds further value to the ongoing assessments. Notably, an article by Matthews Hughes on the support of the Central African Federation under Roy Welensky to the Katanga secessionists offers some insights based on research in the Welensky papers and related archival holdings. Hughes points out that Ndola was a strategically important base for the secessionists and especially the operations by mercenaries, including the presence of Katangan planes (such as the Dornier mentioned above) on the Ndola airfield. In addition, there seemed to be a direct route between Ndola and the Kipushi airfield at the Katangan–Northern Rhodesian border, which mercenaries regularly used. Alport, the British High Commissioner to the Federation of Rhodesia and Nyasaland, complained in December 1961 "that he was never told about improvements to the landing facilities at Kipushi, nor alerted to the fact that camouflaged aeroplanes were visible on the Katangan side of the landing strip", and that "the Federation authorities exercised no control over the arrival and departure of flights".[88] It was also reported by the US State Department "that Tshombe's forces were using Kipushi airfield for logistical support, movement of soldiers, and as a safe-haven for their war-planes".[89] As this article suggests, sifting through the accessible archival hold-ings of individuals who were involved in the events on the ground may offer some further insights into the likely circumstances of the crash.

Unfortunately, the United Nations has no power to mandate the coopera-tion of member states: it can merely request their compliance, relying on the force of its moral authority. Nor is it in a position to call on multinational companies (such as the Belgian Union Minière) to supply any relevant docu-mentation. As a consequence, with no "smoking gun" in sight, doubts remain as to whether the findings of the original investigations were in any way close to what really happened. But this situation can bring no closure. Instead it fuels continued speculation: "To skeptics of the official accounts, the apparent reluctance by the big powers to share all they know with Mr. Othman is inex-plicable, suggesting they are hoping for interest in the case to fade away."[90]

But this will not happen. The genie has already been let out of the bottle. Dag Hammarskjöld and his colleagues will not get their lives back, but those who were close to the deceased still want to know what caused their deaths. It is not by coincidence that family members of some of those who never returned from the mission to Ndola remain active in lobbying support for a continued investigation. The matter now goes far beyond the second Secretary-General.

8

THE LIMITS OF OFFICE

I take pride in belonging to the family of grasses, and I remain quite green in spite of a lot of trampling.[1]

Since Hammarskjöld's legacy lives on, the literature about his life, his achievements and his limitations has not come to an end. We are currently in the midst of a renewed engagement with the "Renaissance man", as Hammarskjöld has been dubbed in the biography posted on the website of the Nobel Prize organisation (which awarded Hammarskjöld the Nobel Peace Prize posthumously in 1961).[2] Hardly any other person in a similar position has been posthumously exposed to as many controversial assessments as he. Evidence of unconditional admiration was present in the reading from Hammarskjöld's writings at the funeral of the journalist Pauline Frederick in May 1990.[3] Others have awarded him a saint-like status.[4] This contrasts with outright condemnation, accusations of his being a docile servant of Western imperialism, who had ultimate personal responsibility for sacrificing Patrice Lumumba by wilfully playing along with his assassination,[5] or dismissals of him as a kind of impostor, as can be found in some more recent academic writings.[6] How emotional and irrational even non-fictional literature can become is illustrated by a recent study, which maintains without any reference to sources:

> Clearly, Hammarskjöld was taking his orders from Belgium as a neocolonial power and from Washington as the leader of the Western powers ... One should give Hammarskjöld the benefit of level-headedness and, thus, presume that his design for the resolution of the Congo crisis, however unfair and diabolic it

might have been, was well examined, though skillfully concealed ... If Lumumba was awkward and politically inexperienced, Hammarskjöld was, in fact, coherently crooked.[7]

As Secretary-General of the United Nations, Dag Hammarskjöld became "a man who has been defamed as few others for good, for bad, and for no reason".[8]

In this last chapter, I want to offer a new approach by applying the perspectives of post-colonial studies. Finally, I revisit some of the appraisals and end with a tribute to a person who died in office during the execution of tasks that he considered a duty.

Empire and White Supremacy

The United Nations, it has been argued by Goetze, "drew mainly on the legal capital of the UN Charter, and on the symbolic capital by past peacekeeping missions as well as Hammarskjöld's personal stature".[9] She summed up further:

> His strong interest in international law, and his propensity to seek out opportunities to fix in writing the rules and procedures of the organization, to document the tasks accomplished and even (before the term became fashionable) the lessons learnt—for instance in the annual reports he introduced—shows that he particularly sought to order the world according to a specific idea of how the rules of the world should be written, and not how the brute force of the states shaped it.[10]

She then moves into somewhat new territory by exploring more closely the sociological structure of peacebuilding during the era of Hammarskjöld and the Congo, and shares a startling observation hardly noticed or pointed out before:

> The default space of peacebuilding is filled with a specific "class" of people. Not everyone can become a peacebuilder, and in the absence of a clearly defined vocational training profile, peacebuilders are more easily identified by social characteristics such as economic or cultural capital than by their profession. The notion of class must be understood in a large sense as a wide category of people who exhibit similar sociological characteristics. The boundaries of classes are fluid and fuzzy, and similarity must not be confused with sameness. The trees in a pine forest provide a useful analogy: they may differ in shape, size and appearance, but they are still pine trees. In the same fashion, the space of peacebuilding is populated by individuals who in their individual outlook are all different, but who, when considered a group, share an important number of

commonalities, most notably with respect to social origins, education, and their related value structure.[11]

An exploration of the sociological characteristics (the "social capital") of those who played a meaningful role in the top executive layer of the Congo mission between 1960 and 1964 shows—not surprisingly—that "education was the prime capital" for building careers in the international civil service. In differing but related ways, the majority of those in the top level could be located "in the (admittedly broad) category of the educated middle classes"— no matter where they came from geographically.[12] "Given the realities of the Cold War, the safest recruitment zones were African or Asian nonaligned countries. However, the geographic distribution obscures the very similar endowments in educational and family-transmitted economic capital, namely the very similar social class origins of the UN staff."[13]

Based on this pattern, Goetze concludes that "Hammarskjöld thus initiated a practice in the UN of appointing his own cabinet, which gave the appearance of reflecting the political and geographic diversity of the UN, yet which was, in reality, based on a close-knit network".[14] As a result, she argues, commonalities in the professional core ideal of the (petty bourgeois or middle-class) "liberal self" were more important than cultural differences might have been, as

> the first generation of peacebuilders understood the civil servant ideal to represent the realization of the liberal, autonomous self. The emphasis was on serving a higher cause and being independent, in the sense of a civil servant who dedicated his (they were almost exclusively men) work life to this noble cause and its organization, the UN. The liberal self was articulated as an intellectually independent person of moral integrity who believes in (liberal and democratic) ideals and selflessly serves a "good" organization in order to fulfil these ideals. Being an international civil servant was a calling, in Weber's sense, that is, a way of fulfilling a moral and ethical duty that was greater than the individual.[15]

This is an important observation: mental dispositions matter. It recalls an invisible form of agency during the processes of decolonisation in which "the intimate enemy" was a contributing factor to the perpetuation of internalised value systems of the previous regime. It means that some conventional anti-colonialism is at the same time able to serve the colonisation of the consciousness.[16] In other words, while Hammarskjöld and his trusted members of staff may have been honest brokers in the search to achieve self-determination, they viewed fundamental structures, norms and values alike without being aware that other perspectives might be as relevant. The perceived shared commonalities among members from different geographical (but not necessarily mental) cultures obscured the awareness that others differed fundamentally from such commonalities. The openness displayed by Hammarskjöld was still part of a view confined to certain boundaries and limitations. Having said that, one must add that this observation is not true of all operating within the institutionalised playing field: "Institutions are social constructions and exist only through the performance of actors in the roles it prescribes. Although a role defines appropriate action, this is not a deterministic model. Actors possess autonomy in the act of interpreting which roles apply to a given situation and what those roles recommend as appropriate."[17]

This means that Hammarskjöld's values and norms were still of importance and by no means only of a secondary nature when he came to deal with decolonisation. A few examples may illustrate this. When opening an exhibition of Asian art in 1956, his remarks indicated the mindset of someone who was willing and able to cross cultural boundaries without any attitude of supremacy:

> It is my conviction that when Asia can speak—as Asia—to the West, and when the West learns to listen and to respond in the spirit of a new and equal relationship, mankind all over the world will profit by it.
>
> Asian nationalism, Asian dynamism and traditionalism—as I said, we often tend to overlook the positive elements in these manifestations of the Asian spirit. Partly we do so because we give to these attitudes interpretations molded on the pattern of our own history, without an ear sufficiently sensitive to the special accent of Asian reactions. We tend to judge the attitudes in terms of our own values or in terms reflecting inherited standards, typical of our special traditions. Our conclusions as to what is right and what is wrong are no more generally valid than similar judgments of what is good and what is bad in the field of arts. A true interchange of ideas and a fruitful collaboration requires that we accept what *is*—is, in its own right—without narrowing our ability to comprehend and appreciate by rigid ideas about what *should be*. This is neither weak acquiescence nor unprincipled tolerance, but a constructive acceptance of the fact that conformity is no more an ideal in international life than it is so within a people, and that there are many equally valid standards for the measurement of human achievement.[18]

Asked over dinner by his friend John Steinbeck what would matter most during a world tour, Hammarskjöld responded: "Sit on the ground and talk to people. That's the most important thing."[19]

When accused of collaborating with the West in the downfall of Lumumba and claiming neutrality in the Congo as a cover-up, he observed that those criticising fell short of engaging with the responsibility "of those major organs of the United Nations which have formulated the mandate". And he added in an almost ironic twist:

> Nor have we, from the same quarters, heard anything about any responsibility for the political leaders in the Congo. On the contrary, when I referred to their responsibility, the comments were that this showed a colonialist attitude. May I ask: who shows respect for a political leader, the one who, like I did, counts on his ability and therefore on his responsibility—in a critical sense or not—or the one who, like my critics in this context, seems to regard the leader as outside any consideration of responsibility?[20]

Admittedly, such views do not transcend the petty bourgeois middle-class mindset that determined to some degree the orientation of top-level staff in ONUC. But they do demonstrate that being an actor within a specific framework does still provide latitude for a variety of perspectives. Given the constraints of the time and the position, it would have been unreasonable to expect a Secretary-General to be more open-minded than Dag Hammarskjöld was. It also recalls the discussion by Mazower in chapter 3 about the discourses during the founding years of the United Nations: "Mazower's emphasis on personalities as creators of internationalist ideas and the leaders of internationalist projects also makes one realize how little import we give to individuals in social sciences. In most contemporary analytical schools studying international politics unique individuals are reduced to political actors behaving in an identical way, calculating their interests, and honing their tactics."[21]

While Dag Hammarskjöld's anti-colonialism was of a specific kind groomed in the tradition of a dominant worldview which had also shaped and permeated the United Nations as a global governance institution, it still represented views and subsequent actions not shared by all in the West. His "whiteness" was a product of empire, but did not necessarily reproduce uncritically and unreflectively the interests of empire. On the other hand, it would be naive to believe that, even if his value system was opposed to certain notions and perspectives of empire and sought to transform it into a fundamentally new global contract, he would have been able to do so. As a review essay on the roles of the Secretary-General in international organisations has commented:

> Of all the variables which scholars have identified affecting the activities, success, and influence of the Secretary-General, probably none—with perhaps the exception of the UN Charter's provisions concerning the office—has been given as much attention as the backgrounds and personal qualities of the incumbents.

The consensus of the authors under review is that while the personal qualities of the officeholders are important, they should be viewed as subsidiary to other variables ... Most importantly, this variable must be placed in its proper perspective in relationship to the nature of the international system.[22]

A Final Tribute

Adekeye Adebajo, a South-African based Nigerian scholar, who is generally sensitive to and critical of Eurocentrism and Western imperialism, has offered a remarkable recognition of Hammarskjöld. While mainly comparing the two African Secretary-Generals, Boutros-Boutros Ghali (as "the pharaoh") and Kofi Annan (as "the prophet"), he characterised Dag Hammarskjöld as the "Southern prophet *par excellence*", who combined this with the role of a "stubborn Pharaoh".[23] As Fröhlich concludes about Hammarskjöld, "much of his success was owing to his firm judgement based on his ethical convictions. The reverse of this was a certain tendency to overestimate the strength of his position and to mistake the political realities of a situation."[24]

Sture Linnér, one of Hammarskjöld's closest staff members, shared this aspect of his character in an interview:

Hammarskjöld's ethical capacity was both his strength and his weakness. Integrity, honesty and character were the basis for all his work. But at the same time he could not understand some procedures of power politics. He could not understand and would not believe that people should be dishonest on very sincere matters and he got indignant about lying. So in a way he was too trusting.[25]

Among the many words in recognition of the legacy created by Hammarskjöld during his lifetime were those of two other colleagues who worked closely with him in the Secretariat. As his legal advisor said:

It may be asked whether an emphasis on principles and legal concepts is not incompatible with the flexibility and adroitness that characterized much of Hammarskjöld's political activity. His technique of fusing those opposing elements—rule and flexibility—into workable solutions is not easily described. It is more art than science ...

It is also of significance in evaluating Hammarskjöld's flexibility that he characteristically expressed basic principles in terms of opposing tendencies (applying, one might say, the philosophic concept of polarity or dialectical opposition). He never lost sight of the fact that a principle, such as that of observance of human rights, was balanced by the concept of non-intervention, or that the notion of equality of states had to be considered in a context which included the special responsibilities of the great Powers. The fact that such precepts had contradictory implications meant that they could not provide automatic answers to particular problems, but rather that they served as criteria which had to be weighed and balanced in order to achieve a rational solution of the particular problem.[26]

And the longest-serving staff member of the United Nations, who joined the organisation in 1945 and worked closely with five Secretary-Generals until his retirement, observed in retrospect:

> Integrity was a quality to which Hammarskjöld attached the highest importance, and it was the keynote of his approach to political and diplomatic action. He would not, indeed could not, undertake an action he thought dishonest or unworthy, and he was thus valued as a friend and interlocutor even by those with whom he strongly disagreed. Within this imperative of integrity, Hammarskjöld was extraordinarily sensitive to the difficulties and sensibilities of the people with whom he was dealing. He had an exceptional talent for suggesting effective solutions that could be accepted without offence by the parties to a conflict. One key to his success as a negotiator was his ability to retain his mobility and to avoid either getting himself boxed in or committing others to rigid public positions that they would have difficulty in changing. By preserving his freedom, he could often make local progress even in situations that appeared hopeless. His keen sense of timing allowed him both to keep alternatives open and, at the right moment, to create new and unexpected options for the parties. In an apparent deadlock he had a talent for spinning a new concept that the conflicting parties might be able to grasp at without losing face.[27]

As Rowan Williams, former Anglican Archbishop of Canterbury, concluded in a review: "Hammarskjöld was one of the most significant moral influences in international politics in the decades immediately after the war", who "almost single-handedly shaped the vision for international co-operation and crisis management that we struggle to realise and, however reluctantly, take for granted across a great deal of the globe ... Hammarskjöld ... told us, as loudly and clearly as he could, that the vision of a world in which interests converge was a necessary exercise of the imagination."[28]

After being reappointed as Secretary-General, Hammarskjöld ended his first speech to staff by citing the opening words of one of his favourite Swedish folksongs, "Will the flowers of joy ever grow?" He then cited the poet Gunnar Ekelöf, who adapted the wording by asking, "Will the day ever come when joy is great and sorrow is small?" and continued:

> Looking at it in terms of humanity, looking at it in terms of the development of human society, it can be said, of course, that what we are trying to do here is to make our small contribution, during our short time, to a development which will finally lead us to the day "when joy is great and sorrow is small."

However, you can also look at those words in a much more personal and intimate sense. I think it is possible to interpret them superficially but it is also possible to interpret them in a sense which goes to the very heart of our way of settling our relation to life. And then I would say that, on the day we feel that we are living with a duty, well fulfilled and worth our while, on that day joy is great and we can look on sorrow as being small.[29]

A word of caution is needed in this final appraisal. Hammarskjöld's ethics have been for obvious reasons a major reference point in most appraisals of him in his role as Secretary-General. After all, they played a central role in his own arguments. As we have seen, his ever-visible moral compass drew very opposite conclusions. He was either praised for his uncompromising values and principles or considered an unscrupulous "fake" moralist. One must, however, resist the temptation to accept his ethics only at face value, independent of the conclusions drawn. As this book has tried to show, the convictions of the Secretary-General of the United Nations can (and should) matter. But they are anything but decisive elements when it comes to steering and navigating an institution of global governance, in which the conflicting, at times antagonistic, interests of influential players are manifest. Like any other leader of an institution with multiple interests and matters at stake, Hammarskjöld was constantly confronted with the limitations of his office. As we know from those with whom he closely interacted, the permanent conflicts requiring the art of diplomacy and the trading of compromises left their marks. Towards the end of his time in office Hammarskjöld showed signs of wear and tear. While he often used the example of a mountaineer to illustrate the uphill battles, he resorted to a similar analogy at the end of 1960:

> The Assembly session had been a disillusioning experience, reflecting certain ugly underlying tendencies and trends in world politics that he was determined to resist from whatever quarter they came. "The job", he wrote to Hans Engen, who was now State Secretary for Foreign Affairs of Norway, "has become a bit like fighting an avalanche; you know the rules—get rid of the skis, don't try to resist but swim on the surface and hope for a rescuer. (Next morning historians will dig up the whole rotten mess and see how many were buried.) A consolation is that avalanches, after all, automatically always come to a stop and that thereafter you can start behaving like an intelligent being again—provided you have managed to keep afloat."[30]

Among the questions that need further investigation is whether Hammarskjöld indeed managed not to be among the buried, but to keep afloat by following his own course and convictions. Another question is the extent to which he was able to rescue and protect what he treasured as substantial core values that would make a difference. We know from his many speeches and writings what his ethical values were. We know where he had to compromise. But we do not know (and may never be able to establish beyond speculation) how much of a difference he really made. All we know is that he was often at loggerheads with some of the most powerful states in global politics, and that he seemed to believe that taking sides with the less influential members of the world community would be in many (if not most) cases the right thing to do. Any tribute should remain modestly reluctant to make final judgements.

Hammarskjöld was fascinated by the novels of Joseph Conrad, his narratives of the inner struggle reflecting "the solitary individual's situation in life", which emphasised "moral and psychological issues, responsibility and duty", and whose key concepts were solidarity and solitude.[31] His last piece of writing, an essay written in Swedish just before his death for the Swedish Tourist Association (whose vice-chairman he was) and published in its yearbook for 1962, recalls his upbringing. He ends with reflections on the annual gathering of former and current graduates awarded doctorates by Uppsala University in a ceremony held at the end of the academic year:

> you can see them—the jubilee doctor, still with the laurel wreath on his brow, and the young one who has just received his degree and is looking forward to his lectureship. There are fifty years between them. One goes over the hill in order to see, once more before leaving, the town where he has spent many a long year laying the foundation of his life's work. The other, about to encounter the town of his youth, measures the distance between what he once hoped for and what he achieved. How many return as victors?
>
> How many come back?[32]

At the end of September 1961, Dag Hammarskjöld's body was laid to rest in the family grave in the town's old cemetery. In an entry in his notebook, he had once declared: "I believe that we should die with decency so that at least decency will survive."[33]

NOTES

1. INTRODUCTION: HISTORY BETWEEN FACT AND FICTION

1. Hammarskjöld, *Markings*, 140 (entry of 22 December 1957).
2. Urquhart, *Hammarskjold*.
3. Most prominently among those Lash, *Dag Hammarskjold*, but also Miller, *Dag Hammarskjold*.
4. Fröhlich, *Dag Hammarskjöld und die Vereinten Nationen*; and *Dag Hammarskjöld as Secretary-General*.
5. Lipsey, *Hammarskjöld*. Lipsey might as an author have engaged with the various dimensions of Hammarskjöld's personality and thinking more deeply and intimately than anyone else. His empathy and identification with him are an open confession of his unreserved admiration.
6. Ask and Mark-Jungkvist (eds.), *The Adventure of Peace*; Stahn and Melber (eds.), *Peace Diplomacy, Global Justice and International Agency*.
7. Most notably Kille, *From Manager to Visionary*, ch. 4.
8. See for further reading and literature some of the chapters in Stahn and Melber (eds.), *Peace Diplomacy, Global Justice and International Agency*.
9. Albeit included in more recent general studies on the Cold War in Africa, such as Namikas, *Battleground Africa*; and Schmidt, *Foreign Intervention in Africa*.
10. O'Malley, *The Diplomacy of Decolonisation*.
11. Goetze, *The Distinction of Peace*.
12. *Ibid.*, 144.
13. I plead guilty of being in some of my earlier writings also a member of such a club.
14. Most prominently O'Brien, *To Katanga and Back*, which serves his own egocentric desire and justification more than giving a fair recognition of Hammarskjöld's role.
15. Sinclair, "The international civil servant in theory and practice", 757.
16. 2,696 pages, to be exact, including notes and comments by the editors as well as indexes. Referenced throughout as Cordier and Foote, vol. II to V.

17. Wachtmeister, "Leader—statesman—friend", 84.
18. Gleijeses, *H-Diplo Roundtable Review*, 7.
19. *Ibid.*
20. Nzongola-Ntalaja, *The Congo from Leopold to Kabila*, 114.
21. Nzongola-Ntalaja, *H-Diplo Roundtable* Review, 15, with reference to Nzongola-Ntalaja, "Ralph Bunche, Patrice Lumumba, and the first Congo crisis".
22. *Ibid.*, 16, with reference to Dayal, *Mission for Hammarskjöld*, 308.
23. Mazov, *A Distant Front in the Cold War*.
24. Nzongola-Ntalaja, *H-Diplo Roundtable Review*, 16.
25. Dayal, *Mission for Hammarskjöld*, 308–9.
26. *Ibid.*, 311.
27. Linnér, "Dag Hammarskjöld and the Congo crisis", 25.
28. *Ibid.*, 26.
29. *Ibid.*

2. SERVICE AS DUTY: DAG HAMMARSKJÖLD'S UPBRINGING, ETHICS, AND EARLY CAREER

1. Hammarskjöld, *Markings*, 3.
2. *Ibid.*, 4.
3. For a concise illustrated portrait of Agnes and Hjalmar Hammarskjöld and their influence on their son Dag, see Berggren, *Dag Hammarskjöld*, 14–33. Subsequent chapters offer further personal, at times intimate, insights into Hammarskjöld's life and the culture of the emerging Swedish welfare state before assuming office at the United Nations.
4. Söderblom (1866–1931) was the Archbishop of Uppsala from 1914 until his death. He received the Nobel Peace Prize in 1930 in recognition of his ecumenical engagement for peace. He occasionally involved the young Dag Hammarskjöld in preparations for events.
5. Her uncle (half-brother to her father) was the famous Swedish writer Carl Jonas Love Almqvist (1793–1866), characterised by Wikipedia as "a romantic poet, early feminist, realist, composer, social critic, and traveller". As an empathetic and spiritual woman, she was the opposite of her controlled, unemotional husband. A fellow undergraduate of Dag described her as "kind-hearted and excitable; one could never be quite sure whether she was laughing or crying; her maternal feelings were so overwhelmingly generous and warm that no one in her circle could escape her restless attentions." Quoted in Berggren, *Dag Hammarskjöld*, 21.
6. *Ibid.*, 33.
7. Bo Hammarskjöld (1891–1974) was a secretary of state and the county governor of Södermanland; Åke Hammarskjöld (1893–1937) was Registrar of the Permanent Court of International Justice at The Hague from 1922 to 1936 and then a judge until his death. Sten Hammarskjöld (1900–1972) was the only one with a less stellar career.

8. Hammarskjöld, *Markings*. The Swedish original was published as *Vägmärken*, which could have—maybe more appropriately—been translated as "Waymarks". For another translation with detailed comments and interpretations as the result of a life-long work, see Erling, *A Reader's Guide to Dag Hammarskjöld's Waymarks*. For copyright reasons it is only freely accessible on the website of the Dag Hammarskjöld Foundation: http://www.daghammarskjold.se/publication/readers-guide-dag-hammarskjolds-waymarks/.

9. His Uppsala years are documented by Thelin, *Dag Hammarskjöld* and Frängsmyr, *Dag Hammarskjöld och Uppsala universitet*. The bond with the place of his upbringing remained throughout his life, though he never spoke to a university audience there, as he did at many other universities. His remains are buried in the Hammarskjöld family grave at Uppsala's old cemetery together with his parents and three brothers, of whom two as mentioned made careers as high-ranking officials in public service.

10. Appelqvist, *A Hidden Duel*. Myrdal (1898–1987) was professor of economics at Stockholms Högskola from 1933–1947, a Social Democratic member of Parliament from 1933 and Minister of Trade (1945–1947). He was Executive Secretary of the United Nations Economic Commission for Europe (1947–1957) before returning to an academic career and becoming internationally acclaimed for his wider socio-economic and humanist (in particular anti-Vietnam War) engagements. While both were considered part of the influential inner circle of economists later dubbed the Stockholm School, he and Hammarskjöld differed fundamentally on Sweden's post-World War II fiscal policy and later also over the priorities in United Nations economic support to newly independent developing countries.

11. A concise overview on Hammarskjöld as influential economist shaping economic and fiscal policy during the 1930s and 1940s is offered by Orford, "Hammarskjöld, economic thinking and the United Nations", 157–74. The Swedish central bank (*Riksbank*) devoted a special issue of its quarterly *Sveriges Riksbank Economic Review* (no. 3/2005) to Hammarskjöld's role in domestic and international economic policy on the occasion of his hundredth birthday, with main articles by Landberg, "Time for choosing"; Appelqvist, "Civil servant or politician?"; and Ahlström and Carlsson, "Hammarskjöld, Sweden and Bretton Woods", covering the distinct stages of his Swedish career. The new Swedish 1,000 kronor bank notes introduced in 2015 display his portrait.

12. Wigforss (1881–1977), member of the left wing in the Social Democratic Workers Party, was finance minister in 1925–1926 and from 1932 to 1949 and a key player in Sweden's social and economic policy.

13. Landberg, "The road to the UN", 32. For a detailed history of Hammarskjöld's career as Swedish civil servant, see Landberg, *På väg*.

14. Undén (1886–1974) was like Wigforss (and Myrdal, for that matter) in the left-

133

wing faction of the Social Democratic Workers Party, a cabinet member without portfolio (1917–1920 and 1932–1936) and foreign minister (1924–1926 and 1945–1962).

15. Landberg, "The road to the UN", 41, summarising Hammarskjöld, "Statstjänstemannen och samhället", *Tiden*, 7, 1951.

16. See Bouman, *Dag Hammarskjöld*, chapters 2 and 3 and Klumpjan, "Eine Synthese zwischen Nation und Welt", 96ff.

17. Klumpjan, "Eine Synthese zwischen Nation und Welt", 96.

18. Hammarskjöld, *Markings*, 31.

19. *Ibid.*, v.

20. Troy, "Dag Hammarskjöld", 438.

21. See Lipsey, *Hammarskjöld*, 592ff.

22. The best examples for linking some entries in *Markings* as comments or reflections to Hammarskjöld's experiences in diplomacy and policy are Fröhlich, *Dag Hammarskjöld und die Vereinten Nationen*, and even more so Lipsey, *Hammarskjöld*. They both show how fruitful it is to read the notebook entries alongside his involvement in events taking place around the same time.

23. Goetze, *The Distinction of Peace*, 146.

24. See the deep analyses of social history in West European societies in transition from late feudalism to early capitalism among others by Elias, *The Court Society* and *The Civilizing Process*; by Foucault, *The Order of Things* and *The Archaeology of Knowledge*; or Hobsbawm's trilogy on the "long nineteenth century" (*The Age of Revolution: Europe 1789–1848*; *The Age of Capital: 1848–1875*; and *The Age of Empire: 1875–1914*), to mention only a few prominent examples.

25. See for example the extensive works of Israel, *Radical Enlightenment*; *Enlightenment Contested*; and *Democratic Enlightenment*.

3. THE UNITED NATIONS BETWEEN EMPIRE AND EMANCIPATION

1. Chapter I/Article 1 from the Charter of the United Nations; accessible with the amendments since then at http://www.un.org/en/charter-united-nations/.

2. For details, see http://www.un.org/en/sections/history-united-nations-charter/ 1941-atlantic-charter/index.html.

3. One of the notable few exceptions is in the Preamble of the Universal Declaration of Human Rights, which refers to faith "in the dignity and worth of the human person and in the equal rights of men and women".

4. The (inconclusive) debates are instructive as to the variety of interpretations the document allowed. On the one side it was maintained that self-determination "is not identical with national self-determination", Hula, "National self-determination reconsidered", Others stressed "that the normative principle of self-determination passed into customary international law through the August 1941 Atlantic Charter", Laing, "The norm of self-determination, 1941–1991", 209. Others again

highlighted "how anticolonial activists in Africa invoked the Atlantic Charter in struggles for self-determination", Ibhawoh, "Testing the Atlantic Charter", 842.

5. Quoted in Ojo, "Africa and the United Nations system", 73.

6. Pearson, "Defending empire at the United Nations", 543.

7. On the origins of the mandate system and trusteeship, see Matz, "Civilization and the mandate system".

8. Pearson, "Defending empire at the United Nations", 541.

9. Kay, "The politics of decolonization", 788–9.

10. Sellström, "The Trusteeship Council", 109; see in more detail Pearson, "Defending empire at the United Nations".

11. Full text accessible at http://www.un.org/en/universal-declaration-human-rights/.

12. Maldonado-Torres, "On the coloniality of human rights", 122.

13. Whelan, *Indivisible Human Rights*, 137. See as examples the case study of Cameroon as a UN trust territory by Terretta, "We had been fooled into thinking that the UN watches over the entire world", and the advocacy of Nnamdi Azikiwe (first President of independent Nigeria) as regards the human rights focus in his anticolonial activism, in Ibhawoh, "Testing the Atlantic Charter", 8–10.

14. Spijkers, *The United Nations*, 10.

15. Full text accessible at https://documents-dds-ny.un.org/doc/RESOLUTION/GEN/NR0/079/80/IMG/NR007980.pdf?OpenElement.

16. Spijkers, *The United Nations*, 382.

17. For a review of some assessments of its relevance and impact, see Wood, "Retrieving the Bandung Conference".

18. In addition, also individuals from African countries, among others Kenya and South Africa, were in attendance, see Eckert, "African nationalists and human rights", 296.

19. Phillips, "Beyond Bandung", 329.

20. See for a summary Burke, *Decolonization and the Evolution of International Human Rights*, ch. 1.

21. Acharya, "Who are the norm makers?", 409–10.

22. Final Communiqué of the Asian-African conference of Bandung (24 April 1955), accessible at http://franke.uchicago.edu/Final_Communique_Bandung_1955.pdf.

23. Acharya, "Who are the norm makers?", 415.

24. Acharya, "Studying the Bandung Conference from a global IR perspective", 354.

25. Accessible in full length at http://www.sahistory.org.za/archive/wind-change-speech-made-south-africa-parliament-3-february-1960-harold-macmillan.

26. Full text accessible at http://www.un.org/en/decolonization/declaration.shtml.

27. Klose, "Human rights for and against empire", 337.

28. Kouassi, "Africa and the United Nations since 1945", 872. The author suggests three—at times overlapping—stages of the United Nations as "benevolent imperialist", as "ally in liberation" and as "partner in development".

29. Klose, "Debating human rights and decolonization", with reference to Klose, *Human Rights in the Shadow of Colonial Violence*, Burke, *Decolonization and the Evolution of International Human Rights*, and Terretta, "We had been fooled into thinking that the UN watches over the entire world".

30. Eckel, "Human rights and decolonization", 113.

31. *Ibid.*, 129.

32. So the title of chapter three by Moyn, *The Last Utopia*, 84–119.

33. *Ibid.*, 8.

34. Moyn, *Human Rights and the Uses of History*, 18.

35. Klose, "Source of embarrassment".

36. Mazower, *Governing the World*.

37. Mazower, "Governing the world".

38. Mazower, *Governing the World*, 256.

39. Mazower, *No Enchanted Palace*, 18.

40. *Ibid.*, 14.

41. *Ibid.*, 10.

42. *Ibid.*, 30–1 and 18.

43. *Ibid.*, 25.

44. See Lloyd, "A most auspicious beginning"; Dubow, "Smuts, the United Nations and the rhetoric of race and rights"; Thakur, "The 'hardy annual'".

45. Mazower, *No Enchanted Palace*, 26.

46. Heyns and Gravett, "To save succeeding generations from the scourge of war", 600.

47. *Ibid.*, 598 and 597.

48. *Ibid.*, 599 and 601.

49. *Ibid.*, 603.

50. *Ibid.*, 605.

51. Kumalo, "The UN. A personal appreciation", 31.

52. Mazower, *No Enchanted Palace*, 14.

4. DAG HAMMARSKJÖLD'S CREDO AND THE UNITED NATIONS

1. "Address at University of California Convocation", Berkeley, California, 13 May 1954, in Cordier and Foote, vol. II, 301.

2. Lie, *In the Cause of Peace*.

3. Ravndal, "A force for peace", 456.

4. *Ibid.*, 448, quoting Report of the Preparatory Commission of the United Nations, UN Doc. PC/20 (23 December 1945), 87.

5. Jones, "Seeking balance", 61.

6. While he has been so far the only Secretary-General to resign, Boutros Boutros-Ghali, serving from 1992 to 1996, was the first Secretary-General who was denied a second term in office because of the US veto.

7. Lie, *In the Cause of Peace*, 76; quoted in Ravndal, "A force for peace", 455.

8. *Ibid.*, 456.

9. Urquhart, *Hammarskjold*, 15.

10. *Ibid.*

11. *Ibid.*, 13.

12. *Ibid.*, 15. See also the not very favourable but entertaining portrait of Lie by Urquhart, "Character sketches", at http://www.un.org/apps/news/infocus/trygvie-lie.asp#.W1mOYq2B3q0. It ends with a summary of the unsavoury smear campaign he pursued against his successor, which was tantamount to character assassination. Despite being deeply offended, Hammarskjöld reportedly handled this obstruction with utmost dignity.

13. Wikipedia offers a fair interpretation: "*Lagom* (pronounced [ˈlɑːɡɔm]) is a Swedish word meaning 'just the right amount'. The *Lexin* Swedish-English dictionary defines *lagom* as 'enough, sufficient, adequate, just right'. *Lagom* is also widely translated as 'in moderation', 'in balance', 'perfect simple', and 'suitable' (in matter of amounts)." See https://en.wikipedia.org/wiki/Lagom. *Lagom* also relates to *jantelagen*, which means not to stick out but to act inside a collective and not to seek special attention or recognition, but consider the group as more important than oneself. See for an explanation of both words as virtues also http://www.muchissaidinjest.com/2011/02/24/swedish-words-zlatan-is-not-lagom/. Put differently, in the motto of the three musketeers: one for all and all for one.

14. Quoted in Lipsey, *Hammarskjöld*, 163.

15. Ignatieff, "The faith of a hero".

16. Hammarskjöld, *Markings*, 71.

17. Highly instructive also is Klumpjan, "Menschheitsanwalt—und Kritiker der Menschenrechtler", which highlights the specific Swedish approach to human rights during the early twentieth century and its reproduction in Hammarskjöld's advocacy.

18. "'Old creeds in a new world'. Written for Edward J. Murrow's radio programme 'This I Believe'", November 1953, in Cordier and Foote, vol. II, 195.

19. "From New Year's message as broadcast over United Nations Radio", New York, 31 December 1953, in Cordier and Foote, vol. II, 209.

20. Bouman, *Dag Hammarskjöld*, 41.

21. "Address before Second Assembly of the World Council of Churches", Evanston, Illinois, 20 August 1954, in Cordier and Foote, vol. II, 352. See also Melber, "Faith as politics—and politics as faith".

22. "Address at Commencement Exercises of Amherst College", Amherst, Massachusetts, 13 June 1954, in Cordier and Foote, vol. II, 306.

23. "Address at Special United Nations Convocation of the University of California", Berkeley, California, 25 June 1955, in Cordier and Foote, vol. II, 519 and 524.

24. "On the Uppsala tradition. From address after receiving honorary degree at Uppsala College", East Orange, NJ, 4 June 1956, in Cordier and Foote, vol. III, 164.

25. *Ibid.*, 164–5.

26. Hammar, "Dag Hammarskjöld and Markings", 113.

27. Lyon, "The UN Charter, the New Testament, and Psalms", 122ff; Troy, "Two 'popes' to speak for the world".

28. Åström, "Dag Hammarskjöld and international law", 9.

29. Goetze, *The Distinction of Peace*, 148.

30. Troy, "Dag Hammarskjöld"; Dionigi, "Dag Hammarskjöld's religiosity and norms entrepreneurship".

31. "Address at a public meeting organized by the United Nations Association at the Royal Albert Hall", London, 17 December 1953, in Cordier and Foote, vol. II, 201.

32. "Meeting at the beginning of his second term", New York, 10 April 1958, in Cordier and Foote, vol. IV, 68.

33. Nelson, "Dag Hammarskjöld's spirituality", 106.

34. A copy of this book was with him on board the plane which crashed on the night of 17/18 September 1961 when approaching Ndola, killing Hammarskjöld and all 15 others in his company.

35. Svegfors, *Dag Hammarskjöld*; see also Bouman, *Dag Hammarskjöld*.

36. "'The world and the nation'. Commencement address at Stanford University", Palo Alto, California, 19 June 1955, in Cordier and Foote, vol. II, 512.

37. "The United Nations: its ideology and activities. Address before the Indian Council of World Affairs", New Delhi, India, 3 February 1956, in Cordier and Foote, vol. II, 660.

38. "Address at Commencement Exercises of Amherst College", Amherst, Massachusetts, 13 June 1954, in Cordier and Foote, vol. II, 302.

39. "'The walls of distrust'. Address at Cambridge University", Cambridge, England, 5 June 1958, in Cordier and Foote, vol. IV, 91–2.

40. "From transcript of press conference", New York, 4 February 1960, in Cordier and Foote, vol. IV, 533.

41. *Ibid.*, 533–4.

42. "'Asia, Africa and the West'. Address before the Academic Association of the University of Lund", Lund, Sweden, 4 May 1959, in Cordier and Foote, vol. IV, 381 and 382.

43. "Remarks at the Metropolitan Museum of Art on the occasion of the opening of a special loan exhibition, 'Asian Artists in Crystal,'" New York, 8 March 1956, in Cordier and Foote, vol. III, 59.

44. "Statement at the Human Rights Day concert", New York, 10 December 1960, in Cordier and Foote, vol. V, 296–7.

45. Hammarskjöld, *Markings*, 48.

46. Goetze, *The Distinction of Peace*, 51.

47. "'International Service'. Address at Johns Hopkins University Commencement Exercises", Baltimore, Maryland, 14 June 1955, in Cordier and Foote, vol. II, 503.

48. *Ibid.* The quote is from *The Discourses of Epictetus*, ch. XXII, "On the calling of the Cynic": "But the Cynic, instead of all these, should have self-respect for his shelter: if he has not that, he will be naked and exposed and put to shame." See http://www.sacred-texts.com/cla/dep/dep081.htm.

49. *Ibid.*, 504.

50. *Ibid.*

51. *Ibid.*, 506.

52. *Ibid.*

53. *Ibid.*, 507.

54. "Address at Special United Nations Convocation of the University of California", Berkeley, California, 25 June 1955, in Cordier and Foote, vol. II, 520.

55. *Ibid.*

56. *Ibid.*

57. *Ibid.*, 523.

58. *Ibid.*

59. Sinclair, "The international civil servant in theory and in practice", 753.

60. See Bring, "Hammarskjöld's dynamic approach to the UN Charter and international law".

61. See also Schachter, "Dag Hammarskjöld and the relation of law to politics".

62. Bring, "Hammarskjöld's dynamic approach to the UN Charter and international law".

63. Schachter, "The international civil servant", 41.

64. Lippmann (1889–1974) was a prominent American writer and journalist, who was among the first to coin the term "Cold War".

65. As quoted by Hammarskjöld in "'The international civil servant in law and in fact'. Lecture delivered in congregation at Oxford University", Oxford, England, 30 May 1961, in Cordier and Foote, vol. V, 471. The full article by Lippmann was originally published in the *New York Herald Tribune* on 17, 18 and 19 April 1961.

66. *Ibid.*, 476.

67. *Ibid.*, 479.

68. *Ibid.*, 484.

69. *Ibid.*, 486–7.

70. *Ibid.*, 488–9. See, for the current relevance of Hammarskjöld's Oxford speech, Corell, "The need for the rule of law in international affairs"; Corell, "Dag Hammarskjöld, the United Nations and the rule of law".

71. "Introduction to the Sixteenth Annual Report", New York, 17 August 1961, in Cordier and Foote, vol. V, 556.

72. "Suez crisis", New York, 31 October 1956, in Cordier and Foote, vol. III, 309.

73. "Introduction to the Fifteenth Annual Report", New York, 31 August 1960, in Cordier and Foote, vol. V, 139.
74. *Ibid.*, 140.
75. "Meeting at the beginning of his second term", New York, 10 April 1958, in Cordier and Foote, vol. IV, 66.
76. Hammarskjöld, *Markings*, 94.
77. Levefer, *Uncertain Mandate*, 30.
78. O'Brien, *To Katanga and Back*, 47. He then adds to the admiration of Hammarskjöld's skilful use of words the ambiguous characterisation: "We even, I think, found something slightly intoxicating in the paradox of equivocation being used in the service of virtue, the thought of a disinterested Talleyrand, a Machiavelli of peace."
79. Gazarian, "Already fifty years ago", 81.
80. Urquhart, "Dag Hammarskjöld", 134.
81. Urquhart, "Dag Hammarskjöld. Fifty years later", 71.
82. "From transcript of press conference", New York, 12 June 1961, in Cordier and Foote, vol. V, 492.
83. "At UN Correspondents' Association luncheon in his honor at the beginning of his second term", New York, 9 April 1958, in Cordier and Foote, vol. IV, 64.
84. Beskow, *Dag Hammarskjöld*, 181.
85. Letter to Uno Willers of 10 February 1961; quoted in Lipsey, "From the unwritten manual", 120.
86. Bring, "The Hammarskjöld approach to international law", 60.
87. Sinclair, "The international civil servant in theory and in practice", 749.
88. "Last words to the staff—from remarks on staff day", New York, 8 September 1961, in Cordier and Foote, vol. V, 563, 564 and 566.
89. Hammarskjöld, *Markings*, 71.
90. "Address at celebration of the 180th anniversary of the Virginia Declaration of Rights", Williamsburg, Virginia, 15 May 1956, in Cordier and Foote, vol. III, 142. The quote is from Ezra Pound, *The Cantos*, Canto XC.

5. DAG HAMMARSKJÖLD, THE COLD WAR, DEVELOPMENT AND AFRICA

1. "Introduction to the Fifteenth Annual Report", New York, 31 August 1960, in Cordier and Foote, vol. V, 124.
2. Miller, *Dag Hammarskjöld*, 324.
3. See Heller, *The United Nations under Dag Hammarskjöld*, 105ff.
4. *Ibid.*, ch. 4.
5. See for plots and practices by high-ranking officials in the US administration the disclosures as regards the role of the brothers John Foster Dulles and Allen Dulles by Kinzer, *The Brothers* and Poulgrain, *The Incubus of Intervention*.

6. See in particular Williams, *Spies in the Congo*. As she concludes: "the Congo's resources, including its uranium, put the newly independent nation at the very heart of Cold War concerns", 259.
7. Namikas, *Battleground Africa*, 21.
8. O'Malley, *The Diplomacy of Decolonisation*, 2.
9. Heller, *The United Nations under Dag Hammarskjöld*, 94.
10. Mazov, *A Distant Front in the Cold War*.
11. Greenwald, *Pauline Frederick Reporting*, 67.
12. *Ibid.*, 174.
13. Lønning, "Politics, morality and religion", 21.
14. "Introduction to the Eighth Annual Report", 15 July 1953, General Assembly Official Records, Eighth Session, Supplement No. 1 (A/2404), in Cordier and Foote, vol. II, 70 and 73.
15. Webster, "Keenleyside", 3.
16. *Ibid.*, 4.
17. *Ibid.*, 3; see also Webster, "Development advisors in a time of Cold War and decolonization". In 1958, Hammarskjöld folded the TAA into the Economic and Social Department of his Secretariat. Keenleyside continued for a few months as Under-Secretary-General for Public Administration to assist in the establishment of OPEX (Operational and Executive Personnel) as one of the forerunners of the United Nations Development Programme (UNDP) established in November 1965. But like the TAA, OPEX remained rather insignificant in terms of its limited budget, though technical assistance became an integral part of the development agency.
18. Executive Secretary of the United Nations Economic Commission for Europe (ECE) between 1947and 1957.
19. From 1947 with the United Nations Economics Department and among others Director of the Economic Division of the United Nations Industrial Development Organization (UNIDO) and the United Nations Research Institute for Social Development (UNRISD).
20. Executive Director of the United Nations Economic Commission for Latin America (ECLA) between 1950 and 1963.
21. "Introduction to the Ninth Annual Report", 21 July 1954,. General Assembly Official Records, Ninth Session, Supplement No. 1 (A/2663), in Cordier and Foote, vol. II, 332.
22. *Ibid.*
23. *Ibid.*, 333.
24. Quoted in Puntigliano and Appelqvist, "Prebisch and Myrdal", 39.
25. Toye and Toye, *The UN and Global Political Economy*, 107; see also Toye and Toye, "How the UN moved from full employment to economic development", as an idea that was widely approved both by the influential member states and appealing to the former colonies.

26. Fukuda-Parr, "Poverty and inequality", 224.

27. "Statement in the Economic and Social Council on the world economic situation", Geneva, 12 July 1955, in Cordier and Foote, vol. II, 563.

28. "'The United Nations in the modern world'. Article in the *Journal of International Affairs*", Columbia University, 1955, in Cordier and Foote, vol. II, 540.

29. *Ibid.*

30. *Ibid.*, 541.

31. "The United Nations: its ideology and activities", Address before the Indian Council of World Affairs, New Delhi, India, 3 February 1956, in Cordier and Foote, vol. II, 669.

32. "Statement in the Economic and Social Council introducing debate on the world economic situation", Geneva, 16 July 1956, in Cordier and Foote, vol. III, 190–1.

33. Heller, *The United Nations under Dag Hammarskjöld*, 102.

34. Urquhart, *Hammarskjold*, 370.

35. *Ibid.*

36. Quoted *ibid.*, 492.

37. Stokke, *The UN and Development*, 79.

38. "The United Nations: its ideology and activities", Address before the Indian Council of World Affairs, New Delhi, India, 3 February 1956, in Cordier and Foote, vol. III, 672.

39. Fukuda-Parr, "Poverty and inequality", 223.

40. These were Senegal, Liberia, Guinea, Ghana, Togo, Nigeria, Cameroon, Republic of the Congo (Brazzaville), the "Belgian Congo", Ruanda-Urundi, Tanganyika, Zanzibar, Kenya, Uganda, Somalia, Ethiopia, Sudan, Egypt, Libya, Tunisia and Morocco.

41. "From transcript of press conference", Dar es Salaam, Tanganyika (Tanzania), 10 January 1960, in Cordier and Foote, vol. IV, 512.

42. "Extemporaneous remarks at inauguration of the Congress for International Cooperation in Africa at the University Institute of Somalia", Mogadishu, Somalia, 14 January 1960, in Cordier and Foote, vol. IV, 515.

43. "Statement at the second Session of the Economic Commission for Africa", Tangier, Morocco, 26 January 1960, in Cordier and Foote, vol. IV, 517.

44. *Ibid.*, 518.

45. *Ibid.*, 519.

46. "From transcript of press conference", New York, 4 February 1960, in Cordier and Foote, vol. IV, 528.

47. *Ibid.*, 529.

48. Ibid., 536.

49. "Statement in the Economic and Social Council on assistance to former trust territories and other newly independent states in Africa", New York, 14 April 1960, in Cordier and Foote, vol. IV, 568.

50. *Ibid.*, 571.
51. "Introduction to the Fifteenth Annual Report", New York, 31 August 1960, in Cordier and Foote, vol. V, 123.
52. *Ibid.*, 126.
53. *Ibid.*, 127.
54. Muschik, "Managing the world", 139–40. For an overview of the development of this "aid architecture" during the 1950s, see Stokke, *The UN and Development*, 85–105.
55. "Introduction to the Sixteenth Annual Report", New York, 17 August 1961, in Cordier and Foote, vol. V, 561.
56. *Ibid.*
57. "Introduction to the Fifteenth Annual Report", New York, 31 August 1960, in Cordier and Foote, vol. V, 125.
58. De Seynes, "An informal retrospection on Dag Hammarskjöld's commitment to economic and social development", 75.
59. *Ibid.*, 71.
60. Fukuda-Parr, "Poverty and inequality", 223.
61. Orford, "Hammarskjöld, economic thinking and the United Nations", 163. See also Orford, *International Authority and the Responsibility to Protect*.
62. *Ibid.*, 175.
63. *Ibid.*, 176.
64. Sinclair, "The international civil servant in theory and practice", 762.
65. Muschik, "Managing the world", 124.
66. "From transcript of press conference held at the headquarters of the International Civil Aviation Organization", Montreal, 30 May 1956, in Cordier and Foote, vol. III, 162.
67. Muschik, "Managing the world", 132.
68. "From transcript of press conference held at the headquarters of the International Civil Aviation Organization", Montreal, 30 May 1956, in Cordier and Foote, vol. III, 162.
69. *Ibid.*, 163.
70. "An international administrative service. Address before the International Law Association at McGill University", Montreal, 30 May 1956, in Cordier and Foote, vol. III, 150 and 151.
71. Muschik, "Managing the world", 135.
72. *Ibid.*, 143.
73. *Ibid.*
74. Rietkerk, *In Pursuit of Development*, 253.
75. Sinclair, "The international civil servant in theory and practice", 764.
76. O'Malley, *The Diplomacy of Decolonisation*, 2; see also O'Malley, "'What an awful body the UN have become!!'"

6. THE SCOPE AND LIMITS OF DAG HAMMARSKJÖLD'S DIPLOMACY

1. Hammarskjöld, *Markings*, 113 (entry of 10 June 1956).
2. But see also, on subsequent limitations of the success with regard to the issue of navigation rights through the canal, Heller, *The United Nations under Dag Hammarskjöld*, 60–4.
3. The chapter draws partly on some of my earlier work: "Dag Hammarskjöld and Africa's decolonisation"; "Mission impossible"; and *Dag Hammarskjöld and Conflict Mediation*.
4. See the analyses by Saunders, "Hammarskjöld's visit to South Africa"; Sellström, "Hammarskjöld and apartheid South Africa"; and Saunders, "Dag Hammarskjöld and apartheid South Africa".
5. See Stultz, "Evolution of the United Nations anti-apartheid regime", 1–4 and 8–9; United Nations/Department of Public Information, *The United Nations and Apartheid*, 9–16.
6. Saunders, "Dag Hammarskjöld and apartheid South Africa", 62.
7. See for details https://www.sahistory.org.za/topic/sharpeville-massacre-21-march-1960.
8. See for more details Stultz, "Evolution of the United Nations anti-apartheid regime", 4ff.
9. See for more details Saunders, "Dag Hammarskjöld and apartheid South Africa", 62ff.
10. Sellström, "Hammarskjöld and apartheid South Africa", 44f.
11. Stultz, "Evolution of the United Nations anti-apartheid regime", 10.
12. For more details see Ruf, "The Bizerta crisis", 206–9.
13. See Cordier and Foote, vol. V, 527–37. For a concise summary of the events unfolding see Heller, *The United Nations under Dag Hammarskjöld*, 78–81.
14. Reproduced in full in Little, *The Poet and the Diplomat*, 123–32.
15. *Ibid.*, 127.
16. See Lipsey, *Hammarskjöld*, 514–21.
17. See ch. 5.
18. Fröhlich, "The 'Suez story'", 305.
19. Goetze, *The Distinction of Peace*, 47.
20. The UN General Assembly had adopted the Uniting for Peace resolution in 1950 with UN A/RES/377(V). It stipulates that, "if the Security Council because of lack of unanimity of the permanent members, fails to exercise its primary responsibility for the maintenance of international peace and security in any case where there appears to be a threat to the peace, breach of the peace, or act of aggression, the General Assembly shall consider the matter with a view to making the appropriate recommendations to the members for collective measures, including in the case of a breach of the peace or act of aggression the use of armed force when necessary to maintain or restore international peace and security."

21. These notes are now accessible in the Dag Hammarskjöld private archives at the Royal Library in Stockholm.

22. Quoted in Fröhlich, "The 'Suez story'", 311.

23. "Suez crisis", New York, 31 October 1956, in Cordier and Foote, vol. III, 309.

24. Deeply frustrated over the inability to deal similarly with the Soviet invasion of Hungary, during deliberations in the Security Council on 4 November 1956, Hammarskjöld said with reference to his speech of 31 October that he wanted to put on record that the same view applied to that situation.

25. Yaqub, "Introduction to review of Laron", 2.

26. Laron, *The Origins of the Suez Crisis*, 12.

27. See in much detail Robertson, *Crisis*.

28. General Assembly Official Records, First Emergency Special Session, Annexes, Document A/3267, subsequently Resolution 999 (ES-I) of 4 November 1956, in Cordier and Foote, vol. III, 318.

29. Quoted in Fröhlich, "The 'Suez story'", 314.

30. General Assembly Resolution 999 (ES-I), 3 November 1956, in Cordier and Foote, vol. III, 320–1. For all details of the frantic diplomacy and unfolding between October and December 1956, see "Settlement of the Suez Canal dispute", in Cordier and Foote, vol. III, 292–411.

31. Fröhlich, "The 'Suez story'", 322–3.

32. Quoted *ibid.*, 334.

33. *Ibid.*, 337.

34. *Ibid.*, 339.

35. For a detailed account see Hoskyns, *The Congo since Independence*, 1–105.

36. Telegram dated 12 July 1960, from the President and the Prime Minister of the Republic of the Congo to the Secretary-General. Security Council Official Records, Fifteenth Year, Supplement for July, August and September 1960, document S/4382, in Cordier and Foote, vol. V, 18–19.

37. *Ibid.*, 19.

38. For a detailed chronology of the events unfolding, see Merriam, *Congo*.

39. "The Secretary-General may bring to the attention of the Security Council any matter which in his opinion may threaten the maintenance of international peace and security."

40. O'Malley, "The Dag factor", 283.

41. "Opening statement in the Security Council", New York, 13 July 1960, in Cordier and Foote, vol. V, 21, 22 and 23.

42. Security Council Official Records, Fifteenth Year, Supplement for July, August and September 1960, document S/4387, *ibid.*, 25.

43. *Ibid.*, 26.

44. Rognoni, "Dag Hammarskjöld and the Congo crisis", 201.

45. Urquhart, *Hammarskjold*, 403–4.

46. "First report on assistance to the Republic of the Congo", New York, 18 July 1960, in Cordier and Foote, vol. V, 29 and 30.

47. "Statement in the Security Council introducing his report", New York, 20 July 1960, *ibid.*, 42.

48. *Ibid.*, 43.

49. *Ibid.*, 44–5.

50. "Summary of composition and deployment of the United Nations force in the Congo", New York, 31 July 1960, *ibid.*, 49–50.

51. "First statement in the Security Council introducing his second report", New York, 8 August 1960, *ibid.*, 71.

52. *Ibid.*

53. "The Members of the United Nations agree to accept and carry out the decisions of the Security Council in accordance with the present Charter."

54. "The Members of the United Nations shall join in affording mutual assistance in carrying out the measures decided upon by the Security Council."

55. Cordier and Foote, vol. V, 76.

56. "Interpretation of paragraph 4 of the Security Council's Third Resolution on the Congo", Léopoldville, Congo, 12 August 1960, *ibid.*, 87.

57. Security Council Official Records, Fifteenth Year, 887th meeting. Quoted *ibid.*, 113.

58. *Ibid.*, 114.

59. *Ibid.*, 120.

60. Mazov, "Soviet aid to the Gizenga government", 427. The supply of equipment turned out to become a nightmare when later the trucks were used to carry the supporters of Lumumba to be executed. *Ibid.*, 428.

61. Zeilig, *Patrice Lumumba*, 114. Little has been published on the specific case of South Kasai, so closely linked to Katanga. While only touching on it in passing, it is however included in an important pointer, which not only contributes to a better understanding of the massacre among the Baluba but also explains in part the Katangese local dynamics beyond the interests of Belgium and the mining companies: "the tendency of his [Lumumba's] supporters to assume the existence of popular support for the new central state and its government in all parts of the country, with no recognition of the evidently uneven and contradictory nature of the Congolese territory and the variable extent to which the people of Congo related to it, is ultimately ahistorical, denying agency to those Africans who adopted a sincerely held opposition to the central state." Kennes and Larmer, *The Katangese Gendarmes*, 42.

62. "Fourth report to the Security Council", New York, 7 September 1960, in Cordier and Foote, vol. V, 158–9.

63. Mazov, "Soviet aid to the Gizenga government", 428.

64. "Opening statement in the Security Council", New York, 9 September 1960, in Cordier and Foote, vol. V, 165.

65. A/L.292/Rev. 1, sponsored by 17 African and Asian states, *ibid.*, 191.

66. "Concluding statement after adoption of Afro-Asian resolution", New York, 19 September 1960, *ibid.*, 193.

67. General Assembly Official Records, Fifteenth Session, 869th plenary meeting. Quoted *ibid.*, 194–5.

68. "Statement of reply to Khrushchev and others during general debate", New York, 26 September 1960, *ibid.*, 197 and 198.

69. "'I shall remain in my post …' Second statement of reply", New York, 3 October, *ibid.*, 200–1. See for visual documentation https://www.youtube.com/watch?v=xEQr_dbH79Q.

70. Mazov, "Soviet aid to the Gizenga government", 432.

71. Urquhart, "UN interview", 22.

72. Urquhart, *Hammarskjold*, 443–4. He refers to Hoskyns, *The Congo since Independence*, 208–10 for a discussion of this constitutional question.

73. Irwin, "Sovereignty in the Congo crisis", 213.

74. Goetze, *The Distinction of Peace*, 49.

75. O'Malley, *The Diplomacy of Decolonisation*, 53, quoting Namikas, *Battleground Africa*, 117.

76. *Ibid.*, 51.

77. The by far most detailed account is offered by De Witte, *The Assassination of Lumumba*.

78. "Letters to President Kasavubu", in Cordier and Foote, vol. V, 238.

79. *Ibid.*, 239–40.

80. "Opening statement in the Security Council", New York, 7 December 1960, *ibid.*, 242, 243, 243–4.

81. "Communications protesting the transfer of Patrice Lumumba to Katanga", New York, January 1961, *ibid.*, 322.

82. Rikhye, "Hammarskjöld and peacekeeping", 106.

83. De Witte, *The Assassination of Lumumba*, xv. This interpretation is shared in tendency by Hintjens and Cruz, "Continuities of violence in the Congo", and to a lesser extent by Tshonda, "Lumumba vs. Hammarskjöld". For a less romanticising appreciation of Lumumba's role and his personality, see Zeilig, *Patrice Lumumba*, who also resists the temptation to blame Hammarskjöld for Lumumba's gruesome killing.

84. Urquhart, "The tragedy of Lumumba".

85. De Witte, "The tragedy of Lumumba. An exchange".

86. Urquhart, "The tragedy of Lumumba".

87. Legum, *Congo Disaster*. Colin Legum (1919–2003) was a widely recognised and respected South African senior journalist. Because of his anti-apartheid convictions, he lived in exile until 1991.

88. Kalb, *The Congo Cables*, 290.

89. Urquhart, "UN interview", 32.
90. O'Brien, *To Katanga and Back*. O'Brien later returned to the Congo as a subject with his controversial play on Lumumba and Hammarskjöld, *Murderous Angels*; see Cohen, "Politics vs drama". For other (partly deviating) perspectives from the ground, see Dayal, *Mission for Hammarskjold*, and Urquhart, *A Life in Peace and War*.
91. Gordenker, "Conor Cruise O'Brien", 908. Brian Urquhart was even less impressed: "I think that book is really not only very self-indulgent—that wouldn't matter— but is also extremely dishonest, because it deliberately distorts a great number of the things that happened in order to make a case for saying that fighting old Conor O'Brien, the true blue hero, was betrayed by this overly cautious, dishonest Swede—which simply isn't the case." For him, the book is "a tissue of nonsense ... it's good fiction but not very good history." Urquhart, "UN interview", 32 and 34.
92. Nzongola-Ntalala, *The Congo from Leopold to Kabila*, 114.
93. Young, "Ralph Bunche and Patrice Lumumba", 127. See also Urquhart, *Ralph Bunche*, ch. 22.
94. Goetze, *The Distinction of Peace*, 80.
95. Nzongola-Ntalala, "Ralph Bunche, Patrice Lumumba, and the first Congo crisis", 156.
96. Collins, "The Cold War comes to Africa", 267.
97. Urquhart, "Character sketches, Patrice Lumumba", 5.
98. Letter to John Steinbeck, 28 February 1961, Dag Hammarskjöld Papers, Royal Library, Stockholm. Quoted in Nelson, *Courage of Faith*, 218 (fn. 734); original emphasis.
99. Urquhart, "UN interview", 25.
100. Kent, *America, the UN and Decolonisation*, 61. See in much detail Muehlenbeck, *Betting on the Africans*.
101. "Second statement after Soviet demand for his dismissal", New York, 15 February 1961, in Cordier and Foote, vol. V, 349–50.
102. Dayal, *Mission for Hammarskjold*, 189–214. Dayal was, as Hammarskjöld's special representative, the head of the United Nations Operation in the Congo between September 1960 and May 1961. His personal account offers details on the interactions on the ground and within the mission.
103. *Ibid.*, 190.
104. Security Council Resolution 161 (1961) of 21 February 1961 (S/4741), in Cordier and Foote, vol. V, 356–7.
105. *Ibid.*, 358.
106. "Statement in the Security Council after adoption of Afro-Asian resolution", New York, 21 February 1961, in Cordier and Foote, vol. V, 359.
107. The stalemate is well illustrated in the chapters 14 ("Vicarious Stewardship") and

15 ("Reluctant Release") in Dayal, *Mission for Hammarskjold*, whose role as special representative ended abruptly in May 1961 because of the blockage.

108. "Third statement", New York, 7 April 1961, in Cordier and Foote, vol. V, 433.

109. "Fourth statement", New York, 18 April 1961, *ibid.*, 437.

110. See Mazov, "Soviet aid to the Gizenga government".

111. See for this period and the unusual blunt intervention the comprehensive documentation in Kalb, *The Congo Cables*, 274–6.

112. Cordier and Foote, vol. V, 540.

113. For details, see the highly personal account of O'Brien, *To Katanga and Back*, 195ff.

114. Cordier and Foote, vol. V, 541.

115. A series of stories and reproduced cables were posted on the web site of *The Guardian*, 17 August 2011.

116. http://www.guardian.co.uk/world/interactive/2011/aug/17/un-cable-hammarskjold-katanga-operation-morthor?INTCMP=SRCH.

117. http://www.guardian.co.uk/world/interactive/2011/aug/17/un-cable-hammarskjold-operation-morthor?INTCMP=SRCH.

118. Quoted in Collins, "Letters show O'Brien had UN authority for actions in Katanga".

119. Scarnecchia, "The Congo crisis", 65.

120. O'Brien, *To Katanga and Back*, 261.

121. "First message to Mr. Tshombé", 16 September 1961, in Cordier and Foote, vol. V, 570.

122. Urquhart, "UN interview", 29.

123. The independent Norwegian researcher Hans Kristian Simensen has discovered such cables, in which Western diplomats expressed their concerns and suspicions about Hammarskjöld's initiative to meet Tshombe for finding a solution, which might have resulted in a loss of Western control over the Katanga province.

124. Gibbs, "Dag Hammarskjold", 174.

125. Fröhlich, "Dag Hammarskjöld", 67.

126. Fröhlich, *Political Ethics and the United Nations*, 191.

127. Legum, *Congo Disaster*, 166ff.

128. "Last words to the staff—from remarks on staff day", New York, 8 September 1961, in Cordier and Foote, vol. V, 564.

129. "Introduction to the Sixteenth Annual Report", New York, 17 August 1961, *ibid.*, 544.

130. *Ibid.*, 545.

131. Namikas, *Battleground Africa*, 226.

132. Schmidt, *Foreign Intervention in Africa*, 64.

133. Linnér, "Dag Hammarskjöld and the Congo crisis", 29.

134. Lefever, *Uncertain Mandate*, 30.

135. *Ibid.*, 220.
136. Outgoing code cable from Hammarskjöld to de Seynes, 19 July 1960, National Library of Sweden, MS L179:155; quoted in Rognoni, "Dag Hammarskjöld and the Congo crisis", 195.
137. Irwin, "Sovereignty in the Congo crisis", 203.
138. Weissman, "What really happened in the Congo", 14.
139. Irwin, "Sovereignty in the Congo crisis", 208.
140. Goetze, *The Distinction of Peace*, 49.
141. It was documented only recently when the General Assembly adopted on 21 December 2016 with 105 votes in favour, 52 abstentions and 15 votes against (including Russia and China) a resolution to establish an investigation into war crimes in Syria—a decision the Security Council would never have been able to take due to the veto power of some of its members.
142. "First statement", New York, 29 March 1961, in Cordier and Foote, vol. V, 420.
143. "Third statement in the Assembly", New York, 19 December 1960, *Public Papers of the Secretaries-General, vol. V*, p. 285.
144. O'Malley, *The Diplomacy of Decolonisation*, 6.
145. Sens, "The newly independent states, the United Nations, and some thoughts on the nature of the development process", 125; see also Jacobson, *The USSR and the UN's Economic and Social Activities*.
146. Jacobson, "ONUC's civilian operations", 102.
147. *Ibid.*, 107.
148. Kouassi, "Africa and the United Nations since 1945", 886.

7. DEATH AT NDOLA

1. Entry by Dag Hammarskjöld into his notebook dated 3 December, 1960. In the English translation by Erling, *A Reader's Guide*.
2. Greenwald, *Pauline Frederick Reporting*, 177.
3. These were Niels-Eric Aahréus, Serge L. Barrau, Francis Eivers, Vladimir Fabry, Per Hallonqvist, S.O. Hjelte, Harold M. Julien, Alice Lalande, Lars Litton, Harold Noork, P.E. Persson, William Ranallo, Karl Erik Rosén, Heinrich A. Wieschhoff and Nils Göran Wilhelmsson.
4. Legum, *Congo Disaster*.
5. Williams, *Who Killed Hammarskjöld?*, 240.
6. For a concise overview on the different speculations, see Fröhlich, "The unknown assignation", 27–33.
7. Williams, *Who Killed Hammarskjöld?* Many of the details presented indicate the extent to which the original investigations were biased, distorted and unwilling to properly examine the evidence.
8. It is partly based on Melber, "The death of Dag Hammarskjöld", and Melber, Wardrop, Williams, "Update. Journey for truth". I thank my fellow musketeers for

their permission to use a few bits of our joint text, which has many more details to offer.

9. In violation of all basic forensic practices, seemingly no photos were taken of his body at the place where it was discovered. The first images only show him on a stretcher.

10. "A substantial amount of evidence thus points to the Secretary-General's body having been found and tampered with well before the afternoon of 18 September and possibly very shortly after the crash." Hammarskjöld Commission, *Report of the Commission of Inquiry*, 17.

11. Notably Von Uexküll, "Hammarskjölds Tod".

12. *New York Times*, "Truman pays tribute to U.N. chief's memory", 20 September 1961.

13. Williams, *Spies in the Congo*.

14. *Ibid.*, 259.

15. See in particular Hughes, "Fighting for white rule in Africa".

16. Kalb, *The Congo Cables*, 297.

17. http://www.guardian.co.uk/world/interactive/2011/aug/17/un-cable-hammarskjold-american-criticism?INTCMP=SRCH.

18. Welensky, *Welensky's 4000 Days*, 238–9.

19. *Ibid.*, 239.

20. Urquhart, "UN interview", 37–8.

21. See also Björkdahl and Phiri, "The Hammarskjöld plane crash", 112.

22. Colvin, *The Rise and Fall*, 88.

23. Federation of Rhodesia and Nyasaland, *Report by the Investigating Board on the Accident to DC6B Aircraft SE-BDY which Occurred near Ndola on 17th September 1961*.

24. Quoted in the Hammarskjöld Commission, *Report of the Commission of Inquiry*, 17–18.

25. Federation of Rhodesia and Nyasaland, *Report of the Commission of Inquiry on the Accident involving Aircraft SE-BDY*, reproduced as No. 33 in ICAO Circular 69-AN/61, 183–190, https://www.baaa-acro.com/sites/default/files/import/uploads/2017/11/SE-BDY.pdf.

26. Many charcoal burners in the forest nearby the crash site were able to make significant observations, which all were either ignored or outright dismissed. For their significant evidence, see Williams, *Who Killed Hammarskjöld?* and Björkdahl and Phiri, "The Hammarskjöld plane crash".

27. United Nations, *Report of the Commission of Investigation*, 66.

28. *Ibid.*, 66–7.

29. https://documents-dds-ny.un.org/doc/RESOLUTION/GEN/NR0/166/81/IMG/NR016681.pdf?OpenElement.

30. https://documents-dds-ny.un.org/doc/RESOLUTION/GEN/NR0/192/67/IMG/NR019267.pdf?OpenElement.

31. Rösiö, *Haveriet vid Ndola.*
32. http://ask.un.org/faq/49766.
33. http://www.hammarskjoldcommission.org/index.html.
34. http://www.hammarskjoldinquiry.info/.
35. Funds were raised through private donations, including substantial amounts by several of the trustees. Other donors included in particular the late Swedish writer Henning Mankell, who made several generous donations but preferred to remain anonymous, the British law professor and author Alexander McCall Smith, and the Barbro Osher Pro Suecia Foundation.
36. The Hammarskjöld Commission, *Report of the Commission of Inquiry,* 19.
37. *Ibid.*
38. *Ibid.,* 27.
39. *Ibid.,* 29.
40. *Ibid.,* 48.
41. *Ibid.,* 36.
42. *Ibid.,* 48.
43. *Ibid.,* 49.
44. *Ibid.,* 48.
45. *Ibid.,* 50.
46. UN News Centre, "Ban to study findings of commission linked to death of former UN chief Hammarskjöld", http://www.un.org/apps/news/story.asp?NewsI D=45803&Cr=hammarskj%C3%B6ld&Cr1=#.UoeU7I2hDdI.
47. Note by the Secretary-General, United Nations, *Investigation into the Conditions and Circumstances,* 21 March 2014, 1 and 2.
48. *Ibid.,* 1.
49. Carlberg, "The search for truth", 11.
50. See for details https://www.robert-schuman.eu/en/doc/oee/oee-1538-en.pdf.
51. 72nd plenary meeting of the UN General Assembly, Monday, 15 December 2014, UN, A/69/PV.72.
52. UN General Assembly, Sixty-ninth Session Agenda, item 128: Investigation into the conditions and circumstances resulting in the tragic death of Dag Hammarskjöld and of the members of the party accompanying him, draft resolution 11 December 2014, A/69/L.42.
53. UN, A/RES/69/246.
54. The other panellists were Kerryn Macaulay, a civil aviation expert and Australia's representative on the Council of the International Civil Aviation Organization (ICAO), and Henrik Ejrup Larsen, a ballistics expert at the National Centre of Forensic Services in the Danish National Police and a member of INTERPOL. See http://www.ipsnews. net/2015/03/u-n-panel-to-investigate-dag-hammarskjolds-death/.
55. Letter of transmittal, United Nations, *Investigation into the Conditions and Circumstances,* 2 July 2015, 5.

56. Letter dated 2 July 2015 from the UN Secretary-General addressed to the President of the General Assembly, *ibid.*, 3.

57. *Ibid.*

58. United Nations, A/70/L.9 https://documents-dds-ny.un.org/doc/UNDOC/ GEN/N15/365/74/PDF/N1536574.pdf?OpenElement.

59. https://papersmart.unmeetings.org/media2/7655383/sweden.pdf.

60. Note by the Secretary-General, United Nations, *Investigation into the Conditions and Circumstances*, 17 August 2016.

61. *Ibid.*, 5.

62. http://www.un.org/en/ga/search/view_doc.asp?symbol=A/RES/71/260.

63. United Nations, *Investigation into the Conditions and Circumstances*, 5 September 2017, 7.

64. See for more details on this revelation Gülstorff, "German links to the Hammarskjöld case".

65. United Nations, *Investigation into the Conditions and Circumstances*, 8.

66. *Ibid.*, 34.

67. *Ibid.*, 38.

68. *Ibid.*, 39.

69. *Ibid.*

70. *Ibid.*, 43.

71. *Ibid.*, 45 and 46.

72. *Ibid.*, 52.

73. *Ibid.*, 50.

74. *Ibid.*, 56.

75. *Ibid.*, 58 and 60.

76. "Letter dated 5 September 2017 from the Secretary-General addressed to the President of the General Assembly", *ibid.*, 2.

77. http://www.un.org/en/ga/search/view_doc.asp?symbol=A/RES/72/252.

78. https://www.un.org/press/en/2018/sga1796.doc.htm.

79. https://www.un.org/press/en/2018/ga12097.doc.htm.

80. *Interim Report of the Eminent Person Appointed Pursuant to General Assembly Resolution 72/252*, unpublished advance copy, 9.

81. *Ibid.*, 4.

82. *Ibid.*, 8.

83. https://www.swedenabroad.se/en/embassies/un-new-york/current/news/swedish-statement-at-the-unga-briefing-on-the-investigation-into-the-conditions-and-circumstances-regarding-the-death-of-dag-hammarsjköld/.

84. Scarnecchia, "The Congo crisis".

85. The Hammarskjöld Commission, *Report of the Commission of Inquiry*, 7.

86. *Ibid.*, 50.

87. Cowell, "UN chief presses to unlock mystery".

88. Hughes, "Fighting for white rule in Africa", 607.
89. *Ibid.*, 611.
90. Cohen and Gladstone, "Do spy agencies hold answer".

8. THE LIMITS OF OFFICE

1. Dag Hammarskjöld in a letter to Bo Beskow, dated 16 March 1957; as quoted in Lipsey, *Hammarskjöld*, 603.
2. https://www.nobelprize.org/nobel_prizes/peace/laureates/1961/hammarskjold-bio.html.
3. Greenwald, *Pauline Frederick Reporting*, 271. Frederick had an "tremendous affection" for Hammarskjöld, *ibid.*, 127. "For the rest of her life Frederick would say that she admired Hammarskjöld more than any of the presidents, politicians, diplomats, or other government officials she had covered", *ibid.*, 113. And she had covered a lot!
4. Lipsey, *Hammarskjöld*.
5. See for example De Witte, *The Assassination of Lumumba*; and Gerard and Kuklick, *Death in the Congo*.
6. See for example Frielingsdorf, *"Machiavelli of Peace"*, Hobbs, *The UN and the Congo Crisis of 1960*, and Larsson, *Bringing Light into the Heart of Darkness?* In contrast, the rather critical assessment by Rietkerk, *In Pursuit of Development*, remains much more convincing for its sound, empirically based approach and measured language.
7. Frindéthié, *From Lumumba to Gbagbo*, 226f.
8. Heller, *The United Nations under Dag Hammarskjöld*, vii.
9. Goetze, *The Distinction of Peace*, 47.
10. *Ibid.*, 148.
11. *Ibid.*, 68.
12. *Ibid.*, 70 and 71.
13. *Ibid.*, 71.
14. *Ibid.*, 83.
15. *Ibid.*, 143.
16. See prominently, and as an early form of the post-colonial school of thought, Nandy, *The Intimate Enemy*.
17. Ravndal, "A force for peace", 444–5.
18. "Remarks at the Metropolitan Museum of Art on the occasion of the opening of a special loan exhibition, 'Asian Artists in Crystal'", New York, 8 March 1956, in Cordier and Foote, vol. III, 60.
19. Quoted in Lind and Thelin, "Nature and culture", 99.
20. "Concluding statement in the Security Council", New York, 13 December 1960, in Cordier and Foote, vol. V, 257–8.

pp. [125–129]

22. Zacher, "The Secretary-General", 938.
23. Adebayo, "The role of the Secretary-General", 92 and 97.
24. Fröhlich, *Political Ethics*, 190.
25. Quoted *ibid.*, 190–1.
26. Schachter, "The international civil servant. Neutrality and responsibility", 48 and 49.
27. Urquhart, "Dag Hammarskjöld. The private person in a very public office", 140–1.
28. Williams, "A review of Hammarskjöld: A Life", 2–3.
29. "Meeting at the beginning of his second term", New York, 10 April 1958, in Cordier and Foote, vol. IV, 68.
30. Urquhart, *Hammarskjold*, 492f.
31. Lind and Thelin, "Nature and culture", 95.
32. Hammarskjöld, *Castle Hill*, 20–1.
33. Hammarskjöld, *Markings*, 142.

155

BIBLIOGRAPHY

Books

Abi-Saab, Georges, *The United Nations Operation in the Congo 1960–1964* (Oxford: Oxford University Press, 1978).

Ask, Sten and Mark-Jungkvist, Anna (eds.), *The Adventure of Peace. Dag Hammarskjöld and the Future of the UN* (New York and Houndsmill: Palgrave Macmillan, 2005).

Berggren, Henrik, *Dag Hammarskjöld. Markings of his Life* (Stockholm: Max Ström, 2016).

Beskow, Bo, *Dag Hammarskjöld: Strictly Personal—A Portrait* (Garden City, NY: Doubleday, 1969).

Bouman, Monica, *Dag Hammarskjöld, Citizen of the World* (Kampen: Ten Have Baarn, 2005).

Burke, Roland, *Decolonization and the Evolution of International Human Rights* (Philadelphia: University of Pennsylvania Press, 2010).

Colvin, Ian, *The Rise and Fall of Moise Tshombe. A Biography* (London: Leslie Frewin, 1968).

Cordier, Andrew W. and Foote, Wilder (eds.), *Public Papers of the Secretaries-General of the United Nations. Volume II: Dag Hammarskjöld 1953–1956* (New York and London: Columbia University Press, 1972).

———, *Public Papers of the Secretaries-General of the United Nations. Volume III: Dag Hammarskjöld 1956–1957* (New York and London: Columbia University Press, 1973).

———, *Public Papers of the Secretaries-General of the United Nations. Volume IV: Dag Hammarskjöld 1958–1960* (New York and London: Columbia University Press, 1974).

———, *Public Papers of the Secretaries-General of the United Nations. Volume V: Dag Hammarskjöld 1960–1961* (New York and London: Columbia University Press, 1975).

Dayal, Rajeshwar, *Mission for Hammarskjold. The Congo Crisis* (London: Oxford University Press, 1976).

De Witte, Ludo, *The Assassination of Lumumba* (London and New York: Verso, 2001).

Elias, Norbert, *The Court Society* (Oxford: Blackwell, 1983).

———, *The Civilizing Process. Sociogenetic and Psychogenetic Investigations.* (Oxford: Blackwell, 2000; revised edition of 1994).

Foucault, Michel, *The Order of Things. An Archeology of the Human Sciences* (London and New York: Routledge, 2000; French original 1966).

———, *The Archaeology of Knowledge* (London and New York: Routledge, 2002; French original 1969).

Frängsmyr, Carl, *Dag Hammarskjöld och Uppsala universitet* (Uppsala: Uppsala Universitet, 2011).

Frindéthié, K. Martial, *From Lumumba to Gbagbo. Africa in the Eddy of the Euro-American Quest for Exceptionalism* (Jefferson, NC: McFarland, 2016).

Fröhlich, Manuel, *Dag Hammarskjöld und die Vereinten Nationen. Die politische Ethik des UNO-Generalsekretärs* (Paderborn: Schöningh, 2002).

———, *Political Ethics and the United Nations. Dag Hammarskjöld as Secretary-General* (London and New York: Routledge, 2008).

Gerard, Emmanuel and Kuklick, Bruce, *Death in the Congo. Murdering Patrice Lumumba* (Cambridge, MA and London: Harvard University Press, 2015).

Goetze, Catherine, *The Distinction of Peace. A Social Analysis of Peacebuilding* (Ann Arbor: University of Michigan Press, 2017).

Greenwald, Marylin S., *Pauline Frederick Reporting. A Pioneering Broadcaster Covers the Cold War* (Sterling, VA: Potomac, 2015).

Hammarskjöld, Dag, *Markings* (New York: Ballantine, 1983; originally published New York: Alfred A. Knopf and London: Faber & Faber, 1964).

Heller, Peter B., *The United Nations under Dag Hammarskjöld, 1953–1961* (Lanham, MD: Scarecrow Press, 2001).

Hobsbawm, Eric, *The Age of Revolution. Europe 1789–1848* (London: Weidenfeld and Nicolson, 1962).

———, *The Age of Capital. 1848–1875* (London: Weidenfeld and Nicolson, 1975).

———, *The Age of Empire. 1875–1914* (London: Weidenfeld and Nicolson, 1987).

Hoskyns, Catherine, *The Congo since Independence* (London: Oxford University Press, 1965).

Israel, Jonathan I., *Radical Enlightenment. Philosophy and the Making of Modernity* (Oxford: Oxford University Press, 2001).

———, *Enlightenment Contested. Philosophy, Modernity, and the Emancipation of Man 1670–1752* (Oxford: Oxford University Press, 2006).

———, *Democratic Enlightenment. Philosophy, Revolution and Human Rights 1750–1790* (Oxford: Oxford University Press, 2011).

Jacobson, Harold K., *The USSR and the UN's Economic and Social Activities* (Notre Dame, IN: University of Notre Dame Press, 1963).

Kalb, Madeleine G., *The Congo Cables. The Cold War in Africa—From Eisenhower to Kennedy* (New York: Macmillan, 1982).

Kennes, Erik and Larmer, Miles, *The Katangese Gendarmes and War in Central Africa* (Bloomington and Indianapolis: Indiana University Press, 2016).

Kent, John, *America, the UN and Decolonisation. Cold War Conflict in the Congo* (London and New York: Routledge, 2010).

Kille, Kent J., *From Manager to Visionary. The Secretary-General of the United Nations* (New York: Palgrave Macmillan, 2006).

Kinzer, Stephen, *The Brothers: John Foster Dulles, Allen Dulles, and Their Secret World War* (New York: St. Martin's Griffin, 2013).

Klose, Fabian, *Human Rights in the Shadow of Colonial Violence. The Wars of Independence in Kenya and Algeria* (Philadelphia: University of Pennsylvania Press, 2013).

Landberg, Hans, *På väg ... Dag Hammarskjöld som svensk ämbetsman* (Stockholm: Atlantis, 2012).

Laron, Guy, *The Origins of the Suez Crisis. Postwar Development Diplomacy and the Struggle over Third World Industrialization, 1945–1956* (Washington, DC: Woodrow Wilson Center Press and Baltimore, MD: Johns Hopkins University Press, 2013).

Lash, Joseph P., *Dag Hammarskjöld. Custodian of the Brushfire Peace* (New York: Doubleday, 1961).

Lefever, Ernest W., *Uncertain Mandate. Politics of the U.N. Congo Operation* (Baltimore, MD: Johns Hopkins Press, 1967).

Legum, Colin, *Congo Disaster* (Harmondsworth: Penguin, 1961).

Lie, Trygve, *In the Cause of Peace: Seven Years with the United Nations* (New York: Macmillan, 1954).

Lipsey, Roger, *Hammarskjöld. A Life* (Ann Arbor: University of Michigan Press, 2013).

Little, Marie-Noëlle (ed.), *The Poet and the Diplomat. The Correspondence of Dag Hammarskjöld and Alexis Leger* (Syracuse, NY: Syracuse University Press, 2001).

Mazov, Sergey, *A Distant Front in the Cold War. The USSR in West Africa and the Congo, 1956–1964* (Stanford, CA: Stanford University Press and Washington, DC: Woodrow Wilson Center Press, 2010).

Mazower, Mark, *No Enchanted Palace. The End of Empire and the Ideological Origins of the United Nations* (Princeton: Princeton University Press, 2009).

———, *Governing the World. The History of an Idea* (London: Penguin, 2012).

Meisler, Stanley, *United Nations. The First Fifty Years* (New York: Atlantic Monthly Press, 1995).

Merriam, Alan P., *Congo. Background of Conflict* (Evanston, IL: Northwestern University Press, 1961).

Miller, Richard L., *Dag Hammarskjold and Crisis Diplomacy* (New York: Oceana Publications, 1961).

Moyn, Samuel, *The Last Utopia. Human Rights in History* (Cambridge: Belknap Press of Harvard University Press, 2010).

———, *Human Rights and the Uses of History* (London and New York: Verso, 2014).

Muehlenbeck, Philip E., *Betting on the Africans. John F. Kennedy's Courting of African Nationalist Leaders* (Oxford and New York: Oxford University Press, 2012).

Namikas, Lise, *Battleground Africa. Cold War in the Congo, 1960–1965* (Washington, DC: Woodrow Wilson Center Press and Stanford, CA: Stanford University Press, 2013).

Nandy, Ashis, *The Intimate Enemy. Loss and Recovery of Self under Colonialism* (Oxford: Oxford University Press, 1984).

Nelson, Paul, *Courage of Faith. Dag Hammarskjöld's Way in Quest of Negotiated Peace, Reconciliation and Meaning* (Frankfurt/Main: Peter Lang, 2007).

Nzongola-Ntalaja, Georges, *The Congo from Leopold to Kabila: A People's History* (London and New York: Zed Books, 2002).

O'Brien, Conor Cruise, *To Katanga and Back. A UN Case History* (New York: Simon & Schuster, 1962).

———, *Murderous Angels* (London: Hutchinson, 1969).

O'Malley, Alanna, *The Diplomacy of Decolonisation. America, Britain and the United Nations during the Congo Crisis 1960–1964* (Manchester: Manchester University Press, 2018).

Orford, Anne, *International Authority and the Responsibility to Protect* (Cambridge: Cambridge University Press, 2011).

Poulgrain, Greg, *The Incubus of Intervention. Conflicting Indonesian Strategies of John F. Kennedy and Allen Dulles* (Selangor: Strategic Information and Research Development Centre, 2015).

Robertson, Terence, *Crisis. The Inside Story of the Suez Conspiracy* (London: Hutchinson, 1965).

Schmidt, Elizabeth, *Foreign Intervention in Africa. From the Cold War to the War on Terror* (Cambridge: Cambridge University Press, 2013).

Stahn, Carsten and Melber, Henning (eds.), *Peace Diplomacy, Global Justice and International Agency. Rethinking Human Security and Ethics in the Spirit of Dag Hammarskjöld* (Cambridge: Cambridge University Press, 2014).

Stokke, Olav, *The UN and Development. From Aid to Cooperation* (Bloomington and Indianapolis: Indiana University Press, 2009).

Svegfors, Mats, *Dag Hammarskjöld. Den förste modern svensken* (Stockholm: Norstedts, 2005).

Thelin, Bengt, *Dag Hammarskjöld: barnet, skolpojken, studenten* (Stockholm: Carlsson, 2005).

Toye, John and Toye, Richard, *The UN and Global Political Economy. Trade, Finance, and Development* (Bloomington and Indianapolis: Indiana University Press, 2004).

BIBLIOGRAPHY

United Nations, Department of Public Information, *The United Nations and Apartheid, 1948–1994* (New York: Department of Public Information, United Nations, 1994).

Urquhart, Brian, *Hammarskjold* (New York: Harper & Row, 1972).

——, *A Life in Peace and War* (New York and London: W.W. Norton, 1987).

——, *Ralph Bunche. An American Odyssey* (New York and London: W.W. Norton, 1993).

Welensky, Roy, *Welensky's 4000 Days. The Life and Death of the Federation of Rhodesia and Nyasaland* (London: Collins, 1964).

Whelan, Daniel J., *Indivisible Human Rights. A History* (Philadelphia: University of Pennsylvania Press, 2010).

Williams, Susan, *Who Killed Hammarskjöld? The UN, the Cold War and White Supremacy in Africa* (London: Hurst 2011; 2nd enlarged edition 2016).

——, *Spies in the Congo. The Race for the Ore That Built the Atomic Bomb* (London: Hurst, 2016).

Zeilig, Leo, *Patrice Lumumba. Africa's Lost Leader* (London: Haus, 2008).

Chapters in Books

Adebayo, Adekeye, "The role of the Secretary-General", in Adebayo, Adekeye (ed.), *From Global Apartheid to Global Village. Africa and the United Nations* (Scottsville: University of KwaZulu-Natal Press, 2009).

Bouman, Monica, "Dag Hammarskjöld and the politics of hope", in Stahn, Carsten and Melber, Henning (eds.), *Peace Diplomacy, Global Justice and International Agency. Rethinking Human Security and Ethics in the Spirit of Dag Hammarskjöld* (Cambridge: Cambridge University Press, 2014).

Bring, Ove, "The Hammarskjöld Approach to International Law", in Melber, Henning and Schoeman, Maxi (eds.), *The United Nations and Regional Challenges in Africa. 50 Years after Dag Hammarskjöld* (Uppsala: The Dag Hammarskjöld Foundation; Development Dialogue, no. 57, 2011).

——, "Hammarskjöld's dynamic approach to the UN Charter and international law", in Stahn, Carsten and Melber, Henning (eds.), *Peace Diplomacy, Global Justice and International Agency. Rethinking Human Security and Ethics in the Spirit of Dag Hammarskjöld* (Cambridge: Cambridge University Press, 2014).

Corell, Hans, "Dag Hammarskjöld, the United Nations and the rule of law in today's world", in Stahn, Carsten and Melber, Henning (eds.), *Peace Diplomacy, Global Justice and International Agency. Rethinking Human Security and Ethics in the Spirit of Dag Hammarskjöld* (Cambridge: Cambridge University Press, 2014).

De Seynes, Philippe, "An informal retrospection on Dag Hammarskjöld's commitment to economic and social development", in Jordan, Robert S. (ed.), *Dag Hammarskjöld Revisited. The UN Secretary-General as a Force in World Politics* (Durham, NC: Carolina Academic Press, 1983).

Eckert, Andreas, "African nationalists and human rights, 1940s–1970s", in Hoffmann, Stefan-Ludwig (ed.), *Human Rights in the Twentieth Century* (Cambridge: Cambridge University Press, 2011).

Fröhlich, Manuel, "The 'Suez story'. Dag Hammarskjöld, the United Nations and the creation of UN peacekeeping", in Stahn, Carsten and Melber, Henning (eds.), *Peace Diplomacy, Global Justice and International Agency: Rethinking Human Security and Ethics in the Spirit of Dag Hammarskjöld* (Cambridge: Cambridge University Press, 2014).

———, "Dag Hammarskjöld, 1953–1961", in Fröhlich, Manuel and Williams, Abiodun (eds.), *The UN Secretary-General and the Security Council* (Oxford: Oxford University Press, 2018).

Fukuda-Parr, Sakiko, "Poverty and inequality. Challenges in the era of globalisation", in Ask, Sten and Mark-Jungkvist, Anna (eds.), *The Adventure of Peace. Dag Hammarskjöld and the Future of the UN* (New York and Houndsmill: Palgrave Macmillan, 2005).

Gazarian, Jean, "Already fifty years ago", in Henley, Mary-Lynn and Melber, Henning (eds.), *Dag Hammarskjöld Remembered. A Collection of Personal Memories* (Uppsala: Dag Hammarskjöld Foundation, 2011).

Hammar, KG, "Dag Hammarskjöld and Markings", in Ask, Sten and Mark-Jungkvist, Anna (eds.), *The Adventure of Peace. Dag Hammarskjöld and the Future of the UN* (New York and Houndsmill: Palgrave Macmillan, 2005).

Hintjiens, Helen M. and Cruz, Serena, "Continuities of violence in the Congo. Legacies of Hammarskjöld and Lumumba", in Stahn, Carsten and Melber, Henning (eds.), *Peace Diplomacy, Global Justice and International Agency: Rethinking Human Security and Ethics in the Spirit of Dag Hammarskjöld* (Cambridge: Cambridge University Press, 2014).

Irwin, Ryan M., "Sovereignty in the Congo crisis", in James, Leslie and Leake, Elisabeth (eds.), *Decolonization and the Cold War. Negotiating Independence* (London: Bloomsbury 2015).

Jones, Dorothy V., "Seeking balance. The Secretary-General as normative negotiator", in Kille, Kent J. (ed.), *The UN Secretary-General and Moral Authority. Ethics and Religion in International Leadership* (Washington, DC: Georgetown University Press, 2007).

Klose, Fabian, "'Source of embarrassment'. Human rights, state of emergency, and the wars of decolonization", in Hoffmann, Stefan-Ludwig (ed.), *Human Rights in the Twentieth Century* (Cambridge: Cambridge University Press, 2011).

Klumpjan, Helmut, "Menschheitsanwalt—und Kritiker der Menschenrechtler: Dag Hammarskjöld, der paradoxe UNO-Generalsekretär", in Huse, Petra and Dette, Ingmar (eds.), *Abenteuer des Geistes. Dimensionen des Politischen* (Baden-Baden: Nomos, 2008).

———, "'Eine Synthese zwischen Nation und Welt.' Dag Hammarskjöld—Der

Weltbürger, der stets ein Schwede blieb", in Fröhlich, Manuel, Klumpjan, Helmut and Melber, Henning, *Dag Hammarskjöld (1905–1961). Für eine friedliche Welt— Ideen und Impulse des zweiten UN-Generalsekretärs* (Frankfurt/Main: Brandes & Apsel, 2011).

Kouassi, Edmund Kwam, "Africa and the United Nations", in Mazrui, Ali A. (ed.), *UNESCO General History of Africa. Vol. 8: Africa since 1935* (Oxford: Heinemann and Paris: UNESCO, 1993).

Kumalo, Dumisani S., "The UN. A personal appreciation", in Le Pere, Garth and Samasuwo, Nhamo (eds.), *The UN at 60. A New Spin on an Old Hub* (Midrand: Institute for Global Dialogue, 2006).

Landberg, Hans, "The road to the UN. The emergence of the international civil servant", in Ask, Sten and Mark-Jungkvist, Anna (eds.), *The Adventure of Peace. Dag Hammarskjöld and the Future of the UN* (New York and Houndsmill: Palgrave Macmillan, 2005).

Lind, Per, and Thelin, Bengt, "Nature and culture. Two necessities of life", in Ask, Sten and Mark-Jungkvist, Anna (eds.), *The Adventure of Peace. Dag Hammarskjöld and the Future of the UN* (New York and Houndsmill: Palgrave Macmillan, 2005).

Lipsey, Roger, "From the unwritten manual", in Stahn, Carsten and Melber, Henning (eds.), *Peace Diplomacy, Global Justice and International Agency. Rethinking Human Security and Ethics in the Spirit of Dag Hammarskjöld* (Cambridge: Cambridge University Press, 2014).

Lyon, Alynna J., "The UN Charter, the New Testament, and Psalms. The moral authority of Dag Hammarskjöld", in Kille, Kent J. (ed.), *The UN Secretary-General and Moral Authority. Ethics and Religion in International Leadership* (Washington, DC: Georgetown University Press, 2007).

Matz, Nele, "Civilization and the mandate system under the League of Nations as origin of trusteeship", in von Bogdandy, Armin and Wolfrum, Rüdiger (eds.), *Max Planck Yearbook of United Nations Law*, vol. 9 (Leiden: Brill, 2005).

Melber, Henning, "Dag Hammarskjöld and Africa's decolonisation", in Stahn, Carsten and Melber, Henning (eds.), *Peace Diplomacy, Global Justice and International Agency. Rethinking Human Security and Ethics in the Spirit of Dag Hammarskjöld* (Cambridge: Cambridge University Press, 2014).

———, Wardrop, David and Williams, Susan, "Update. Journey for truth—From 2011 to 2016", in Williams, Susan, *Who Killed Hammarskjöld?* (London: Hurst, 2016).

Nelson, Paul R., "Dag Hammarskjöld's spirituality and the quest for negotiated peace, reconciliation and meaning", in Stahn, Carsten and Melber, Henning (eds.), *Peace Diplomacy, Global Justice and International Agency. Rethinking Human Security and Ethics in the Spirit of Dag Hammarskjöld* (Cambridge: Cambridge University Press, 2014).

Nzongola-Ntalala, Georges, "Ralph Bunche, Patrice Lumumba, and the first Congo crisis", in Hill, Robert A. and Keller, Edmond J. (eds.), *Trustee for the Human Community. Ralph J. Bunche, the United Nations, and the Decolonization of Africa* (Athens, OH: Ohio University Press, 2010).

O'Malley, Alanna, "The Dag factor. How quiet diplomacy changed the role of the Secretariat during the Congo crisis, 1960–1961", in Stahn, Carsten and Melber, Henning (eds.), *Peace Diplomacy, Global Justice and International Agency. Rethinking Human Security and Ethics in the Spirit of Dag Hammarskjöld* (Cambridge: Cambridge University Press, 2014).

Orford, Anne, "Hammarskjöld, economic thinking and the United Nations", in Stahn, Carsten and Melber, Henning (eds.), *Peace Diplomacy, Global Justice and International Agency. Rethinking Human Security and Ethics in the Spirit of Dag Hammarskjöld* (Cambridge: Cambridge University Press, 2014).

Rikhye, Indar Jit, "Hammarskjöld and peacekeeping", in Jordan, Robert S. (ed.), *Dag Hammarskjöld Revisited. The UN Secretary-General as a Force in World Politics* (Durham, NC: Carolina Academic Press, 1983).

Rognoni, Maria Stella, "Dag Hammarskjöld and the Congo crisis, 1960–1961", in Stahn, Carsten and Melber, Henning (eds.), *Peace Diplomacy, Global Justice and International Agency. Rethinking Human Security and Ethics in the Spirit of Dag Hammarskjöld* (Cambridge: Cambridge University Press, 2014).

Saunders, Chris, "Dag Hammarskjöld and apartheid South Africa", in Melber, Henning and Schoeman, Maxi (eds.), *The United Nations and Regional Challenges in Africa. 50 Years after Dag Hammarskjöld* (Uppsala: The Dag Hammarskjöld Foundation; Development Dialogue, no. 57, 2011).

Schachter, Oscar, "The international civil servant. Neutrality and responsibility", in Jordan, Robert S. (ed.), *Dag Hammarskjöld Revisited. The UN Secretary-General as a Force in World Politics* (Durham, NC: Carolina Academic Press, 1983).

Sellström, Tor, "The Trusteeship Council. Decolonisation and liberation", in Adebayo, Adekeye (ed.), *From Global Apartheid to Global Village. Africa and the United Nations* (Scottsville: University of KwaZulu-Natal Press, 2009).

Skidelsky, Robert, "Dag Hammarskjöld's assumptions and the future of the UN", in Ask, Sten and Mark-Jungkvist, Anna (eds.), *The Adventure of Peace. Dag Hammarskjöld and the Future of the UN* (New York and Houndsmill: Palgrave Macmillan, 2005).

Tharoor, Shashi, "'The most impossible job' description", in Chesterman, Simon (ed.), *Secretary or General? The Role of the United Nations Secretary-General in World Politics* (Cambridge: Cambridge University Press, 2007).

Tshonda, Jean Omasombo, "Luumba vs. Hammarskjöld. A story of confrontation", in Stahn, Carsten and Melber, Henning (eds.), *Peace Diplomacy, Global Justice and International Agency. Rethinking Human Security and Ethics in the Spirit of Dag Hammarskjöld* (Cambridge: Cambridge University Press, 2014).

Urquhart, Brian, "Dag Hammarskjöld. The private person in a very public office", in

Jordan, Robert S. (ed.), *Dag Hammarskjöld Revisited. The UN Secretary-General as a Force in World Politics* (Durham, NC: Carolina Academic Press, 1983).

———, "Dag Hammarskjöld. Fifty years later", in Henley, Mary-Lynn and Melber, Henning (eds.), *Dag Hammarskjöld Remembered. A Collection of Personal Memories* (Uppsala: Dag Hammarskjöld Foundation, 2011).

Wachtmeister, Wilhelm, "Leader—statesman—friend", in Henley, Mary-Lynn and Melber, Henning (eds.), *Dag Hammarskjöld Remembered. A Collection of Personal Memories* (Uppsala: Dag Hammarskjöld Foundation, 2011).

Young, Crawford, "Ralph Bunche and Patrice Lumumba. The fatal encounter", in Hill, Robert A. and Keller, Edmond J. (eds.), *Trustee for the Human Community. Ralph J. Bunche, the United Nations, and the Decolonization of Africa* (Athens, OH: Ohio University Press, 2010).

Journal Articles

Acharya, Amitav, "Who are the norm makers? The Asian-African Conference in Bandung and the evolution of norms", *Global Governance*, 20(2014), 405–417.

———, "Studying the Bandung Conference from a global IR perspective", *Australian Journal of International Affairs*, 70, 4 (2016), 342–357.

Ahlström, Göran, and Carlsson, Benny, "Hammarskjöld, Sweden and Bretton Woods", *Sveriges Riksbank Economic Review*, 3 (2005), 50–81.

Appelqvist, Örjan, "Civil servant or politician? Dag Hammarskjöld's role in Swedish government policy in the forties", *Sveriges Riksbank Economic Review*, 3 (2005), 13–32.

Björkdahl, Göran and Phiri, Jacob, "The Hammarskjöld plane crash", *International Peacekeeping*, 20, 1 (2013), 98–115.

Cohen, Michael A., "Politics vs drama in O'Brien's 'murderous angels'", *Contemporary Literature*, 16, 3 (1975), 340–352.

Collins, Carole J.L., "The Cold War comes to Africa. Cordier and the 1960 Congo crisis", *Journal of International Affairs*, 47, 1 (1993), 243–269.

Dionigi, Filippo, "Dag Hammarskjöld's religiosity and norms entrepreneurship. A postsecular perspective", *Politics and Religion*, 9, 1 (2016), 162–186.

Dubow, Saul, "Smuts, the United Nations and the rhetoric of race and rights", *Journal of Contemporary History*, 43, 1 (2008), 45–74.

Eckel, Jan, "Human rights and decolonization. New perspectives and open questions", *Humanity*, Fall 2010, 111–135.

Erk, Jan, "Mark Mazower, *Governing the World*" (book review), *Leiden Journal of International Law*, 27 (2014), 797–800.

Fröhlich, Manuel, "The John Holmes Memorial Lecture. Representing the United Nations—individual actors, international agency, and leadership", *Global Governance*, 20, 2 (2014), 169–193.

Gibbs, David N., "Dag Hammarskjöld, the United Nations, and the Congo crisis 1960–1. A reinterpretation", *Journal of Modern African Studies*, 31, 1 (1993), 163–174.

Gordenker, Leon, "Conor Cruise O'Brien and the truth about the United Nations", *International Organization*, 23, 4 (1969), 897–913.

Heyns, Christof and Gravett, Willem, "'To save succeeding generations from the scourge of war'. Jan Smuts and the ideological foundations of the United Nations", *Human Rights Quarterly*, 39 (2017), 574–605.

Hughes, Matthew, "Fighting for white rule in Africa. The Central African Federation, Katanga, and the Congo crisis, 1968–1965", *International History Review*, 25, 3 (2003), 592–615.

Hula, Erich, "National self-determination reconsidered", *Social Research*, 10, 1 (1943), 1–21.

Ibhawoh, Bonny, "Testing the Atlantic Charter. Linking anticolonialism, self-determination and universal human rights", *International Journal of Human Rights*, 18, 7–8 (2014), 842–860.

Jacobson, Harold Karan, "ONUC's civilian operations. State-preserving and state-building", *World Politics*, 17, 1 (1964), 75–107.

Kay, David A., "The politics of decolonization. The new nations and the United Nations political process", *International Organization*, 21, 4 (1967), 786–811.

Klose, Fabian, "Human rights for and against empire. Legal and public discourses in the age of decolonisation", *Journal of the History of International Law*, 18 (2016), 317–338.

Laing, Edward A., "The norm of self-determination, 1941–1991", *California Western International Law Journal*, 22, 2 (1992), 209–308.

Landberg, Hans, "Time for choosing. Dag Hammarskjöld and the Riksbank in the thirties", *Sveriges Riksbank Economic Review*, 3 (2005), 13–32.

Lipsey, Roger, "Dag Hammarskjöld and *Markings*. A reconsideration", *Spiritus. A Journal of Christian Spirituality*, 11, 1 (2011), 84–103.

Lloyd, Lorna, "'A most auspicious beginning'. The 1946 United Nations General Assembly and the question of the treatment of Indians in South Africa", *Review of International Studies*, 16, 2 (1990), 131–153.

Maldonado-Torres, Nelson, "On the coloniality of human rights", *Revista Crítica de Ciências Sociais*, 114 (2017), 117–136.

Mazov, Sergei, "Soviet aid to the Gizenga government in the former Belgian Congo (1960–61) as reflected in Russian archives", *Cold War History*, 7, 3 (2007), 425–437.

Melber, Henning, "Dag Hammarskjöld, the United Nations and Africa", *Review of African Political Economy*, 39, 131 (2012), 151–159.

———, "The death of Dag Hammarskjöld", *Review of African Political Economy*, 41, 141 (2014), 458–465.

——, "Faith as politics—and politics as faith. Beyers Naudé and Dag Hammarskjöld", *Journal for Contemporary History*, 40, 2 (2015), 96–109.

——, "Mission impossible. Hammarskjöld and the UN mandate for the Congo (1960–1961)", *African Security*, 10, 3–4 (2017), 254–271.

Muschik, Eva-Maria, "Managing the world. The United Nations, decolonization, and the strange triumph of state sovereignty in the 1950s and 1960s", *Journal of Global History*, 13 (2018), 121–144.

O'Malley, Alanna, "'What an awful body the UN have become!!' Anglo-American–UN relations during the Congo crisis, February–December 1961", *Journal of Transatlantic Studies*, 14, 1 (2016), 26–46.

Ojo, M. Adeleye, "Africa and the United Nations system. Decolonization and development", *Présence Africaine*, 119 (1983), 72–89.

Pearson, Jessica Lynne, "Defending empire at the United Nations. The politics of international colonial oversight in the era of decolonisation", *Journal of Imperial and Commonwealth History*, 45, 3 (2017), 525–549.

Phillips, Andrew, "Beyond Bandung. The 1955 Asian-African Conference and its legacies for international order", *Australian Journal of International Affairs*, 70, 4 (2016), 329–341.

Puntigliano, A. Rivarola and Appelqvist, Örjan, "Prebisch and Myrdal. Development economics in the core and on the periphery", *Journal of Global History*, 6 (2011), 29–52.

Ravndal, Ellen Jenny, "'A force for peace'. Expanding the role of the UN Secretary-General under Trygve Lie, 1946–1953", *Global Governance*, 23 (2017), 443–459.

Ruf, Werner Klaus, "The Bizerta crisis. A Bourguibist attempt to resolve Tunisia's border problems", *Middle East Journal*, 25, 2 (1971), 201–211.

Saunders, Chris, "Hammarskjöld's visit to South Africa", *African Journal of Conflict Resolution*, 11, 1 (2011), 15–34.

Scarnecchia, Timothy, "The Congo crisis, the United Nations, and Zimbabwean nationalism, 1960–1963", *African Journal of Conflict Resolution*, 11, 1 (2011), 63–86.

Schachter, Oscar, "Dag Hammarskjöld and the relation of law to politics", *American Journal of International Law*, 56, 1 (1962), 1–8.

Sellström, Tor, "Hammarskjöld and apartheid South Africa. Mission unaccomplished", *African Journal of Conflict Resolution*, 11, 1 (2011), 35–62.

Sens, Andrew D., "The newly independent states, the United Nations, and some thoughts on the nature of the development process", *Journal of Politics*, 30, 1 (1968), 114–136.

Stultz, Newell N., "Evolution of the United Nations anti-apartheid regime", *Human Rights Quarterly*, 13, 1 (1991), 1–23.

Terretta, Meredith, "'We had been fooled into thinking that the UN watches over the entire world'. Human rights, UN trust territories and Africa's decolonization", *Human Rights Quarterly*, 34, 2 (2012), 329–360.

Thakur, Vireet, "The 'hardy annual'. A history of India's first UN resolution", *India Review*, 16, 4 (2017), 401–429.

Toye, John and Toye, Richard, "How the UN moved from full employment to economic development", *Commonwealth and Comparative Politics*, 44, 1 (2006), 16–40.

Troy, Jodok, "Dag Hammarskjöld. An international civil servant uniting mystics and realistic diplomatic engagement", *Diplomacy and Statecraft*, 21, 3 (2010), 434–450.

———, "Two 'popes' to speak for the world. The Pope and the United Nations Secretary General in world politics", *Review of Faith and International Affairs*, 15, 4 (2017), 67–78.

Von Uexküll, Gösta, "Hammarskjölds Tod. Text der Fernseh-Reportage vom NDR Hamburg vom Dezember 1961", *Frankfurter Hefte. Zeitschrift für Kultur und Politik*, 17, 5 (1962), 323–332.

Webster, David, "Development advisors in a time of Cold War and decolonization. The United Nations Technical Assistance Administration, 1950–59", *Journal of Global History*, 6, 2 (2011), 249–272.

Weissman, Stephen R., "What really happened in Congo. The CIA, the murder of Lumumba, and the rise of Mobutu", *Foreign Affairs*, 93, 4 (2014), 14–24.

Williams, Rowan, "A review of Hammarskjöld: A Life", *Cambridge Humanities Review*, 3, Lent term 2013, 2–3.

Wood, Sally Percival, "Retrieving the Bandung Conference ... moment by moment", *Journal of Southeast Asian Studies*, 43, 3 (2012), 523–530.

Zacher, Mark W., "The Secretary-General. Some comments on recent research", *International Organization*, 23, 4 (1969), 932–950.

Theses and Other Texts

Appelqvist, Örjan, "A hidden duel. Gunnar Myrdal and Dag Hammarskjöld in economics and international politics 1935–1955" (Stockholm: Stockholm University/ Department of Economic History 2008; Stockholm Papers in Economic History, 2).

Åström, Sverker, "Dag Hammarskjöld and international law in the world today", in Linnér, Sture and Åström, Sverker, *UN Secretary-General Hammarskjöld. Reflections and Personal Experiences. The 2007 Dag Hammarskjöld Lecture* (Uppsala: Dag Hammarskjöld Foundation, 2008).

Carlberg, Ingrid, "The search for truth. Why the United Nations is considering to reopen the investigation into the 1961 death of Secretary General Dag Hammarskjöld", *Dagens Nyheter*, 5 November 2014, http://www.ingridcarlberg.se/ wp-content/uploads/2015/08/The-Search-for-Truth-DN-May–11th-2014.pdf.

Collins, Stephen, "Letters show O'Brien had UN authority for actions in Katanga", *Irish Times*, 13 November 2018, https://www.irishtimes.com/news/politics/ letters-show-o-brien-had-un-authority-for-actions-in-katanga-1.3695184.

Corell, Hans, "The need for the rule of law in international affairs. Reflections on Dag Hammarskjöld's address at Oxford University on 30 May 1961, 'The international civil service in law and in fact'", in Corell, Hans, Lønning, Inge and Melber, Henning, *The Ethics of Hammarskjöld* (Uppsala: Dag Hammarskjöld Foundation, 2010).

Cowell, Alan, "UN chief presses to unlock mystery of Dag Hammarskjöld's death", *International New York Times*, 6 September 2016.

Cowell, Alan and Gladstone, Rick, "Do spy agencies hold answer to Dag Hammarskjold's death? U.N. wants to know", *New York Times*, 15 July 2017.

De Witte, Ludo, "The tragedy of Lumumba. An exchange", *New York Review of Books*, 20 December 2001.

Erling, Bernhard, *A Reader's Guide to Dag Hammarskjöld's Waymarks* (Uppsala: Dag Hammarskjöld Foundation, 2011), http://www.daghammarskjold.se/publication/readers-guide-dag-hammarskjolds-waymarks/.

Frielingsdorf, Per-Axel, "'Machiavelli of peace'. Dag Hammarskjöld and the political role of the Secretary-General of the United Nations", PhD thesis, Department of International Relations, London School of Economics, 2016.

Fröhlich, Manuel, "The unknown assignation. Dag Hammarskjöld in the papers of George Ivan Smith", in Fröhlich, Manuel and Little, Marie-Noëlle, *Beyond Diplomacy. Perspectives on Dag Hammarskjöld* (Uppsala: The Dag Hammarskjöld Foundation, 2008; Critical Currents no. 2).

Gleijeses, Piero, *H-Diplo Roundtable Review*, 12, 28 (2011), 6–8.

Guardian, "UN cable 7 September 1961. Legal doubts over Operation Morthor: Hammarskjöld's own legal advisor raises questions over whether the UN's dramatic intervention in Katanga would be legitimate", 17 August 2011, www.theguardian.com/world/interactive/2011/aug/17/un-cable-hammarskjold-katanga-operation-morthor.

Gülstorff, Torben, "German links to the Hammarskjöld case. Making the case for another possible murder weapon", *Lobster*, no. 76, Winter 2018, https://www.lobster-magazine.co.uk/free/lobster76/lob76-hammarskjold-case.pdf.

Hammarskjöld, Dag, *Castle Hill* (Uppsala: The Dag Hammarskjöld Foundation, 2000).

Hammarskjöld Commission, The, *Report of the Commission of Inquiry*, The Hague, 9 September 2013, amended on 15 September 2013, http://www.hammarskjoldcommission.org/report/.

Ignatieff, Michael, "The faith of a hero", *New York Review of Books*, 7 November 2013, https://www.nybooks.com/articles/2013/11/07/dag-hammarskjold-faith-hero/.

Klose, Fabian, "Debating human rights and decolonization", *Imperial and Global Forum*, 18 February 2014, https://imperialglobalexeter.com/2014/02/18/debating-human-rights-and-decolonization/.

Larsson, Mats, "Bringing light into the heart of darkness? A study of United Nations

Secretary-General Dag Hammarskjöld's role as mediator during the Congo crisis 1960–1961", MA thesis, Department of History, Stockholm University, 2017.

Lederer, Edith M., "New information has emerged on the mysterious plane crash that killed the head of the U.N. in 1961", Associated Press, 3 December 2018, http://time.com/5470013/hammarskjold-un-plane-crash/.

Legum, Colin, "The tragedy of Lumumba. An exchange", *New York Review of Books*, 20 December 2001.

Linnér, Sture, "Dag Hammarskjöld and the Congo crisis, 1960–61", in Linnér, Sture and Åström, Sverker, *UN Secretary-General Hammarskjöld. Reflections and Personal Experiences. The 2007 Dag Hammarskjöld Lecture* (Uppsala: Dag Hammarskjöld Foundation, 2008).

Lønning, Inge, "Politics, morality, and religion. The legacy of Dag Hammarskjöld", in Corell, Hans, Lønning, Inge and Melber, Henning, *The Ethics of Hammarskjöld* (Uppsala: Dag Hammarskjöld Foundation, 2010).

Melber, Henning, "Dag Hammarskjöld and Conflict Mediation" (Pretoria: University of Pretoria/Centre for Mediation in Africa, February 2016, Mediation Arguments, no. 10).

Orford, Anne, "The past as law or history? The relevance of imperialism for modern international law" (New York: Institute for International Law and Justice, New York University of Law 2012; IILJ Working Paper 2012/2).

Rietkerk, Aaron Dean, "In pursuit of development. The United Nations, decolonization and development aid, 1949–1961", PhD thesis, Department of International History, London School of Economics, 2015.

Rösiö, Bengt, *Haveriet vid Ndola—En förnyad granskning.* Swedish Foreign Ministry, Stockholm, 4 March 1993.

Simms, Brendan, "Governing the world. The history of an idea", *The Independent*, 17 November 2012.

Spijkers, Otto, *The United Nations, the Evolution of Global Values and International Law*, PhD thesis, University of Leiden (Cambridge: Intersentia, 2011).

United Nations, *Report of the Commission of Investigation into the Conditions and Circumstances resulting in the Tragic Death of Mr. Dag Hammarskjöld and of Members of the Party Accompanying Him*, General Assembly, A/5069, 24 April 1962, http://repository.un.org/handle/11176/173445.

———, *Investigation into the Conditions and Circumstances resulting in the Tragic Death of Dag Hammarskjöld and of the Members of the Party Accompanying Him*, General Assembly, Sixty-eighth session. Agenda item 175, A/68/800, 21 March 2014.

———, *Investigation into the Conditions and Circumstances resulting in the Tragic Death of Dag Hammarskjöld and of the Members of the Party Accompanying Him*, General Assembly, Seventieth session. Item 130 of the preliminary list (A/70/50), A/70/132, 2 July 2015.

———, *Investigation into the Conditions and Circumstances resulting in the Tragic Death of Dag Hammarskjöld and of the Members of the Party Accompanying Him*, General Assembly, Seventieth session. Agenda item 129, A/70/1017, 17 August 2016.

———, *Investigation into the Conditions and Circumstances resulting in the Tragic Death of Dag Hammarskjöld and of the Members of the Party Accompanying Him*, General Assembly, Seventy-first session. Agenda item 130, A/71/1042, 5 September 2017.

Urquhart, Brian, "UN interview", 19 October 1984 (interviewer: Leon Gordenker), corrected copy (typed manuscript), UNST/DPI/Oral History (02)/U79, UN Library, UN/SA Collection, 20 April 1994, https://digitallibrary.un.org/record/477973?ln=en.

———, "Character sketches, Trygve Lie", UN News Centre, undated, http://www.un.org/apps/news/infocus/trygvie-lie.asp#.W1mOYq2B3q0.

———, "Character sketches, Patrice Lumumba", UN News Centre, undated, http://www.un.org/apps/news/infocus/patrice-lumumba.asp#.W2QUlq2B3-Y.

———, "The tragedy of Lumumba", *New York Review of Books*, 4 October 2001.

Webster, David, "Keenleyside, Hugh Llewellyn", *IO BIO, Biographical Dictionary of Secretaries-General of International Organizations*, ed. by Reinalda, Bob, Kille, Kent J. and Eisenberg, Jaci, www.ru.nl/fm/iobio.

Yaqub, Salim, Introduction to review of Laron, G, *The Origins of the Suez Crisis. Postwar Development Diplomacy and the Struggle over Third World Industrialization, 1945–1956* (Woodrow Wilson Center Press, Washington, DC, and Johns Hopkins University Press, Baltimore, MD), *H-Diplo Roundtable Review*, 16, 15 (23 January 2015), www.tiny.cc/Roundtable-XVI-15.

ACKNOWLEDGEMENTS

Many have accompanied me on the way into and through this book. I would like to acknowledge a few of them. I am grateful to the other "musketeers", with whom I have been involved since 2012 in efforts to come closer to the truth of what really happened on that fatal night of 17/18 September 1961 near Ndola: Susan Williams, Hans-Kristian Simensen and David Wardrop, with Gervase Hood, Roger Lipsey and Inga-Lill Hammarskjöld as part of the extended musketeer family.

I appreciate the recognition and support of Henrik Hammargren, the current executive director of the Dag Hammarskjöld Foundation, who shares with me the commitment to keep the Hammarskjöld values alive. I am also grateful to the other staff at the Foundation's Secretariat, in particular Karin Abbor-Svensson, who is in charge of promoting the Hammarskjöld legacy. They all make me feel welcome to remain on board and to join them occasionally in activities as a senior advisor. I also fondly remember Sven Hamrell, for decades executive director of the Foundation until 1995, who so generously welcomed and supported me at the Foundation.

I am grateful to Iina Soiri and her colleagues at the Nordic Africa Institute, who provided me, as the Institute's previous research director and current senior research associate, with a supportive and pleasant working environment without which I would have been unable to deliver many of the outcomes of my work during the last few years.

I also treasure the collaboration with my colleagues Maxi Schoeman at the University of Pretoria and Heidi Hudson at the University of the Free State in Bloemfontein, who both took the initiative to secure my affiliation to their institutions as extraordinary professor.

ACKNOWLEDGEMENTS

I thank Philip Murphy, Sue Onslow and Mandy Banton, with whom I interact as senior research fellow at the Institute of Commonwealth Studies/ Centre for Advanced Study at the University of London. This affiliation means a lot to me, in view of the Institute's role during the days when solidarity with the struggles for liberation in Southern Africa mattered.

Special thanks go to the Centre of Excellence: Cultural Foundations of Social Integration at the University of Konstanz, which hosted me for the third time (after 2013 and 2015) in April/May 2018 in a wonderful environment so that I could concentrate on this book, among other things.

I owe much to Michael Dwyer and his team at Hurst. They never indicated any doubt that I would deliver and even announced the book at a time when the manuscript was not yet in sight—as if this was of any comfort to me! I hope they do not feel let down by the result I have delivered. Its final version benefited from some very constructive observations by two competent reviewers. I thank them for their fair assessments. I am also grateful to Russell Martin for his professional language editing.

I remember with gratitude the personal encounters and exchanges I had with Jean Gazarian, Knut Hammarskjöld, Per Lind, Sture Linnér, Wilhelm Wachtmeister and Sverker Åström. Having interacted with Hammarskjöld, they were a source of inspiration. I would therefore like to dedicate this work to their memory and that of "the boss", as the Secretary-General was fondly called by his staff.

Most importantly, this publication, like so many others before, would not have been possible without the never-ending support of Sue. I cannot thank her enough for her labour of love: for her care, understanding, patience and tolerance, when more often than usual "the light was on but nobody was at home" because I was once again deeply absorbed in thought. This book, therefore, is as much hers as it is mine.

INDEX